W9-ASR-494

THE LITERARY ART
OF
Edward Gibbon

Oxford University Press, Amen House, London E.C.4

GLASGOW NEW YORK TORONTO MELBOURNE WELLINGTON
BOMBAY CALCUTTA MADRAS KARACHI KUALA LUMPUR
CAPE TOWN IBADAN NAIROBI ACCRA

© *Oxford University Press 1960*

31085

THE LITERARY ART OF Edward Gibbon

BY

HAROLD L. BOND

ASSOCIATE PROFESSOR OF ENGLISH
DARTMOUTH COLLEGE
HANOVER, NEW HAMPSHIRE

OXFORD
AT THE CLARENDON PRESS
1960

PRINTED IN GREAT BRITAIN

TO MY MOTHER
AND THE MEMORY OF
MY FATHER

PREFACE

My indebtedness to earlier students of Gibbon, particularly for biographical materials, will be apparent to all readers; but I should like to mention as especially helpful the excellent biographies by D. M. Low and G. M. Young as well as the splendid edition of Gibbon's Letters by J. E. Norton and the very useful edition of Gibbon's Autobiography by G. B. Hill. J. B. Bury's monumental edition of *The Decline and Fall* I have used throughout.

This study was originally prepared as a dissertation for the Ph.D. degree at Harvard under the direction of Professors Walter J. Bate and the late Hyder E. Rollins. To Professor Bate for his valuable suggestions and encouragement and to Professor Rollins for his careful correction of my original typescript I shall always be grateful. The study has been extensively revised since then, and a number of my friends and colleagues at Dartmouth have helped me by reading large portions of the work at various stages of the revision. I should mention especially Professor Emeritus Henry Dargan and Professor James D. McCallum, the first for his encouragement and criticisms, and the second for his scrupulous reading of much of the text. Professor Harry Schultz, who read my typescript in the early stages of its revision, has also been extremely helpful. To Dartmouth College for relieving me of some of my teaching duties to work on this study I am deeply indebted. But to my wife Nancy, who sacrificed much and helped greatly, typing drafts, revisions, and final copy, go my greatest thanks. In a very real sense the book belongs to us both.

H. L. B.

Hanover, N.H.
10 *July* 1959

CONTENTS

I · THE CONCEPTION

The History of the Decline and Fall of the Roman Empire, by Edward Gibbon, is one of the great historical works of the Western world. Since the publication of the first volume in 1776 generations of readers have derived entertainment and instruction from this monumental creation. Its accuracy as history has withstood the erosion of time remarkably well. Later research has turned up materials which were unavailable to Gibbon, and certainly the history of the Christian Church and of Byzantium has been undertaken by more sympathetic writers; yet the guidance from the age of the Antonines to the threshold of modern Europe which Gibbon offers his readers is generally trustworthy, and it is always illuminating. As Carlyle says: 'Gibbon is a kind of bridge that connects the antique with the modern ages. And how gorgeously does it swing across the gloomy and tumultuous chasm of those barbarous centuries. . . . The perusal of his work forms an epoch in the history of one's mind.'[1] Such different personalities as Byron, Shelley, Cardinal Newman, Abraham Lincoln, Winston Churchill, and Arnold Toynbee have been influenced and in part formed by an early reading of *The Decline and Fall*. Gibbon will continue to be read so long as men are curious about their past, so long as a study of what man has been can be helpful in understanding what man is and might be.

Although studies of Gibbon have been numerous, insufficient attention has been paid to the literary qualities of his great history. It is my purpose to examine *The Decline and Fall* as one of the significant artistic accomplishments of English humanism. The work bears unmistakable marks of the age in which it was written; it also contains elements which transcend its period and give it lasting value among the permanent conquests of the human spirit. It is the thesis of my study that in composing *The Decline and*

[1] Quoted by George B. Hill, ed., *The Memoirs of the Life of Edward Gibbon* (New York, 1900), pp. 335–6.

Fall, Gibbon aspired to write and did in fact write an historical epic. He set himself the task of recording the successive steps in the fall of the great empire of Rome; but he wrote as a 'philosophic historian', one who has something to say about the nature and destiny of man; and he wrote at a time when history was still considered an art. In his long search for a suitable topic, in his twenty-year dedication to his great task, in the scrupulous accuracy and the extreme care which he lavished on the execution of all the parts of his history, he sought pre-eminence among historians. Just as Milton was the first Englishman to write a great epic in verse, so Gibbon aspired to be the first of his countrymen to write an historical epic in prose. The desire for fame was the spur for both men. Milton dedicated his energies to God and to the celebration of His providence. Gibbon, living in a secular age, dedicated his energies to the celebration of his own civilization and the triumph of human reason.

In his famous autobiography he has described the moment in which he first conceived the plan for his history. It was on his first visit to Rome in the year 1764, he writes: 'as I sat musing amidst the ruins of the Capitol, while the bare-footed fryars were singing vespers in the Temple of Jupiter, that the idea of writing the decline and fall of the city first started to my mind. But my original plan was circumscribed to the decay of the city rather than of the empire, and though my reading and reflections began to point towards that object, some years elapsed, and several avocations intervened, before I was seriously engaged in the execution of that laborious work.'[2] Although this is a retrospective passage, dramatically coloured by the successful historian reflecting on a moment of singular importance in his life, there can be no question that his first visit to Rome was crucial in the plan for the great history.

I should like to survey briefly some of Gibbon's more important intellectual activities prior to this visit in order to explain why the study of the fall of Rome became the chief undertaking of his life and his sole bid for fame. It is impossible in short compass to give even a superficial account of his intellectual growth, for perhaps the most impressive feature of his mind is its astonishing erudition. The carefully chosen and well-read books in Gibbon's library

[2] *Memoirs*, p. 167.

amounted to between 6,000 and 7,000 volumes. His one-time fiancée, Suzanne Curchod, says quite justly that his great work 'has been enlarged by the torrents of thought of all ages',[3] and his excellent biographer, G. M. Young, fixes his place in European letters accurately when he writes that Gibbon applied the mind of the eighteenth to the learning of the seventeenth century.[4] But recognizing that we are dealing with a titan, a severe selection of that biographical material most relevant to the question of how he came to choose Rome for his topic will be a useful preliminary to a study of his literary art.

Like the young John Milton, Gibbon was primarily self-educated. At a very early age, under the guidance of his aunt, Mrs. Catherine Porten, he developed a love of reading and a hunger for knowledge which never left him. By the age of twelve he had read Pope's *Homer*, Dryden's *Virgil*, Ovid's *Metamorphoses*, and a large but indiscriminate collection of poetry, romance, history, and travels which he found in his grandfather's library. These early adventures of his mind were without direction or purpose, however, and he arrived at Oxford when he was fifteen with a large stock of heterogeneous erudition. He had made the acquaintance of the Greek and Latin historians in translations and discovered Eachard's Roman history. Before he was sixteen he had read everything in English about the Arabs, Persians, Tartars, and Turks. His tutor at Oxford failed to provide him with either guidance or instruction, and the 'blind activity of idleness' led to what appears to be one of the two spiritual crises of his life. He was converted to Roman Catholicism. His outraged father immediately made arrangements to have him sent to Lausanne where, it was hoped, association with Protestant teachers and friends would expedite his departure from the Roman fold. Gibbon allows to M. Pavilliard, the Calvinist minister with whom he stayed in Lausanne, some credit for his return to Protestantism, but he claims that his own private studies and reflections were largely responsible. In addition to theology, he studied the System of Logic by the now almost forgotten Lausanne scholar, M. de Crousaz. This work may be praised, Gibbon says, 'as a clear and methodical abridgement of the art of reasoning, from our simple ideas to the

[3] Quoted by G. M. Young, *Gibbon* (Edinburgh, 1932), p. 133.
[4] Ibid., p. 72.

most complex operations of the human understanding'.[5] Having mastered it, he turned the new instrument on his Catholic opinions. Lord Sheffield, Gibbon's lifelong friend, has recorded the result: 'M. Pavilliard has described to me the astonishment with which he gazed on Mr. Gibbon standing before him: a thin little figure with a large head, disputing and urging, with the greatest ability, all the best arguments that had ever been used in favour of popery.'[6] Gibbon had impetuously bewildered himself into Catholicism; he carefully reasoned himself out of it. The whole experience was one of the most influential of his life, for he learned from his bruises. He met with the masters of theological controversy over the most important of subjects, his own beliefs; and in confronting their arguments with his own, he began to discover some of the powers of his mind.

Along with this formative experience came a sense of direction and purpose in his studies. Most literary men can recall with pleasure the time and place of the discovery that the serious business of life is educating oneself. For Gibbon this took place at Lausanne. Assigned study gave way to voluntary labours. His appetite for knowledge outstripped his ability to satisfy it. His range of reading, already great, widened and deepened. He practised the art of double translation, which English humanists since the time of Roger Ascham have encouraged. Gradually his Latin began to approach the model of Cicero. His own testimony on his studies will help us understand some of the spirit with which he later viewed Rome. His remarks on Cicero alone deserve special emphasis: 'I read with application and pleasure *all* the epistles, *all* the orations, and the most important treatises on rhetoric and philosophy; and as I read, I applauded the observation of Quintilian, that every student may judge of his own proficiency, by the satisfaction which he receives from the Roman orator. I tasted the beauties of language, I breathed the spirit of freedom, and I imbibed from his precepts and examples the public and private sense of a man.'[7] Long after this time, when he was writing his famous chapter on Roman jurisprudence, and after he had described much of the long descent from the virtue and freedom

[5] *The Autobiographies of Edward Gibbon*, John Murray, ed. (London, 1896), p. 136.

[6] Ibid., p. 136, n.

[7] *Memoirs*, p. 92.

which marked the heroic days of Rome, he recaptures some of the excitement he must have felt when he first read most of Cicero. 'Although I have devoted myself to write the annals of a declining monarchy', he writes, 'I shall embrace the occasion to breathe the pure and invigorating air of the republic.'[8] The Ciceronian spirit of freedom and Cicero's understanding of what constitutes the public and private sense of a man stayed with Gibbon all his life. On his visit to Rome these ideas were foremost in his mind, and they underlie the huge fabric of *The Decline and Fall.*

Cicero and Tacitus, and later Homer, Herodotus, and Xenophon, one would add, were Gibbon's favourite authors; but the young scholar wished to master all of Roman literature.

> After finishing this great Author [i.e. Cicero], a library of eloquence and reason, I formed a more extensive plan of reviewing the Latin Classics under the four divisions of (1) Historians, (2) Poets, (3) Orators, and (4) Philosophers, in a Chronological series, from the days of Plautus and Salust to the decline of the language and empire of Rome; and this plan, in the last twenty-seven months of my residence at Lausanne (January 1756–April 1758), I *nearly* accomplished. Nor was this review, however rapid, either hasty or superficial. I indulged myself in a second and even a third perusal of Terence, Virgil, Horace, Tacitus, etc., and *studied to imbibe the sense and spirit most congenial to my own.*[9]

This passage from the autobiography is partially confirmed by the entries in Gibbon's *Journal* for the period. His studies of Latin literature, although interrupted in April of 1758, did not cease; and six years later when he walked about the forum, he was able to appreciate with the sense and spirit of a Roman senator the tremendous fall from greatness apparent in the gigantic ruins of the city. It was at Lausanne also that Gibbon began reading Homer in Greek, and we learn from later remarks that the author of the *Iliad* and the *Odyssey* was for him as for Cicero the fountain-head of culture. Homer wrote *their* Old Testament.

The classics of Greece and Rome were not the only concern of his studies at Lausanne. He devoted considerable attention to the work of such eminent moderns as Locke, Bayle, Voltaire, Fon-

[8] *The History of the Decline and Fall of the Roman Empire*, J. B. Bury, ed. (7 vols., London, 1896–1900), iv. 442.

[9] *Autobiographies*, pp. 139–40. Last italics mine.

tenelle, and Montesquieu. These men were the great teachers of the eighteenth century. Gibbon was, of course, influenced by them, for he was keenly aware of the leading ideas and intellectual currents of his time. Three writers should be singled out for special emphasis, however. From a study of Bayle, whom Ernst Cassirer calls 'the originator of the ideal of historical accuracy',[10] Gibbon developed a lifelong respect for facts. He praises Bayle for his wonderful power of assembling doubts and objections. He also notes Bayle's technique of turning the arguments of disputants against each other, a technique used so successfully in the study of religious controversy. Gibbon is even more indebted to Montesquieu. He pays him a warm tribute in his autobiography, and he is the only contemporary writer quoted at length in the text of *The Decline and Fall.* It was Montesquieu's discovery that causation in history can depend as much on climate and geography, on the nature of political institutions, or on economic laws, as on the actions of rulers and the genius of generals. Montesquieu's understanding of impersonal causes in history is important here, for Gibbon was the first great historian to make use of this notable advance in historical study. The influence of Voltaire is considerable also. His *Essay on Manners* broadened the scope of history to include the entire culture of a people or a nation. Gibbon later calls him 'a bigot, an intolerant bigot',[11] and in another connexion he remarked that 'the incredulity of this age is often as blind as the faith of its ancestors';[12] but Voltaire's view of history as a drama of the progress of the human mind from a state of barbarism towards a millennium of rational happiness was useful to Gibbon, as will be seen when we consider 'the argument' of *The Decline and Fall.* There are three other 'moderns' whom he mentions as important in the development of the historian of the Roman empire:

1. From the Provincial Letters of Pascal, which almost every year I have perused with new pleasure, I learned to manage the weapon of grave and temperate irony, even on subjects of Ecclesiastical solemnity. 2. The life of Julian, by the Abbé de la Bléterie, first introduced

[10] *The Philosophy of the Enlightenment,* F. C. A. Koelln and J. P. Pettegrove, trans. (Princeton, 1951), p. 206.

[11] *The Decline and Fall,* vii. 139, n. 15.

[12] D. M. Low, *Edward Gibbon* (London, 1937), p. 131.

me to the man and the times. . . . 3. In Giannone's Civil history of Naples I observed with a critical eye the progress and abuse of sacerdotal power, and the Revolutions of Italy in the darker ages.[13]

Readers of *The Decline and Fall* will remember the important role Gibbon assigns to Julian the Apostate as well as the significance he attaches to the growth and abuse of sacerdotal power. Nor should we forget that in the progress of Gibbon's mind, the expansion of literary power accompanied the development of his historical consciousness; the weapon of grave and temperate irony is one of the keenest in the historian's arsenal.

To these experiences the aspiring man of letters added the acquaintance of some of Europe's literary and scholarly dignitaries. He met Voltaire, for whom he then had an excessive admiration; he initiated correspondence with university professors, and he undertook the composition of an essay on the study of literature. It was at this time that he had the only serious love-affair of his life. Suzanne Curchod was later to become the wife of the French minister of finance, Jacques Necker. When Gibbon met her in 1757 she was a well-educated, charming, and vivacious girl of twenty, the only child of a country minister. The attachment between the two seems to have become deep and genuine, but their plans for marriage were futile in the face of adamant opposition from Gibbon's father. The well-known sentence in the autobiography, 'I sighed as a lover; I obeyed as a son', compresses and dispatches the youthful anguish and despair which Gibbon must have felt when, on his return to England in 1758, his father flatly refused even to consider his son's marriage to this 'foreigner'. Gibbon was to see her occasionally in later life and to re-establish on the basis of friendship the relationship which was founded on passion; but the wounds of this affair could be healed only by severe discipline of his emotions, and the scars lasted.

The years at Lausanne were the most important and formative ones of his life, as Gibbon himself well realized. 'Such as I am in Genius or learning or manners, I owe my creation to Lausanne: it was in that school that the statue was discovered in the block of marble. . . .'[14] The statue is that of a citizen of Europe. He returned to his native land, a maturing scholar with an awakened mind.

[13] *Autobiographies*, p. 143.

[14] Ibid., p. 152.

His emotional and spiritual struggles were quieted by a growing awareness of his own intellectual power, and he was already ambitious to gain a reputation in letters. The energy and diligence with which he applied himself to Roman literature are characteristic of his studies of contemporary works; but one may say of him what he has said of Alexander Severus: 'The works of Virgil and Horace, the republics of Plato and Cicero, formed his taste, enlarged his understanding, and gave him the noblest ideas of man and government.'[15] His values were firmly grounded in classical humanism, and he found little reason to change or modify them throughout the rest of his life. The citizen of Europe needed one important experience, however, before he could also be an Englishman. Two years' service in the Hampshire militia may have been unpleasant for the young scholar, but it gave him a knowledge of his own country and people. The captain of the Hampshire Grenadiers became a soldier as well as an Englishman, and the years spent on this duty were not useless, he says, to the historian of the Roman legions.

The period between his return to England in 1758 and his entrance into the militia in 1761 afforded him considerable leisure. Although part of this time was employed in completing his *Essai sur l'étude de la littérature*, much more was spent in reading English authors. He was especially fond of Swift and Addison and other writers since the revolution, for 'they breathe the spirit of reason and liberty', and they helped him regain facility in the use of English. It was during this time that he first read the histories of Scotland and of the Stuarts, by Robertson and Hume. He tells us in his autobiography that he aspired from early youth to the character of an historian, and on his return to England these aspirations must have been intensified. Hume's great history had been published in 1754–9; Robertson's first volume reached the public in 1759. Gibbon has described his sentiments on reading these works: 'The perfect composition, the nervous language, the well-turned periods of Dr. Robertson, inflamed me to the ambitious hope that I might one day tread in his footsteps: the calm philosophy, the careless inimitable beauties of his friend and rival, often forced me to close the volume with a mixed sensation of delight and despair.'[16] There is no doubt that he hoped to make

[15] *The Decline and Fall*, i. 151.

[16] *Autobiographies*, p. 167.

a third in the select company of British historians, so recently formed. Hume and Robertson had already met the old reproach that Great Britain had produced no major works of history, and in 1761 Gibbon began to examine possible topics for his initial effort. He recorded his dedication to history in a journal entry made at camp, near Winchester, 26 July of the same year:

> My own inclination as well as the taste of the present age have made me decide in favour of history. Convinced of its merit my reason cannot blush at the choice. But this is not all. Am I worthy of pursuing a walk of literature which Tacitus thought worthy of him, and of which Pliny doubted whether he was himself worthy? The part of an historian is as honourable as that of a mere chronicler or compiler of gazettes is contemptible. For which task I am fit, it is impossible to know until I have tried my strength; and to make the experiment, I ought soon to choose some subject of history which may do me credit, if well treated; and whose importance, even though my work should be unsuccessful, may console me for employing too much time in a species of composition for which I was not well qualified.[17]

Meanwhile, he had completed and published his *Essai.* This work contains some information which throws light on the manner in which he approached the study of history. The purpose of the essay is to demonstrate that all the faculties of the mind may be exercised and displayed by the study of ancient literature, the classics of Greece and Rome. Apart from Gibbon's defence of the classics, what particularly concerns us is his definition of the 'philosophe', especially the philosophic historian. This is the role that the author of *The Decline and Fall* assumed when he undertook his great work. The philosophic historian finds in the varied spectacle of human affairs universal principles, the secret springs of action, which render intelligible all ages and times. Assuming, as did most of his contemporaries, the uniformity of human nature, Gibbon goes on to say that those who know the writings of Cicero, Tacitus, Bacon, Fontenelle, and Montesquieu will have a good understanding of what he is trying to describe.

> The philosophic spirit consists in the ability to go back to fundamental ideas; to grasp and unite first principles. The perception of the 'philosophe' is exact, but at the same time broad. Placed on a

[17] *The Miscellaneous Works of Edward Gibbon*, John, Lord Sheffield, ed. (2nd ed., 5 vols., London, 1814), v. 487.

height, he takes in a great extent of country, of which he forms a precise and unique image; while minds just as exact, but more limited, can perceive only a part of the same area. He might be a geometrician, an antiquary, a musician, but he is always a 'philosophe'; and by the strength of penetrating the first principles of his art, he becomes superior to it. He has a place among that small number of geniuses who, coming at long intervals, work to form that primary science, to which, should it be perfected, the others would be subject.[18]

The power of the philosophe is an intellectual gift, he adds, but among those so equipped mentally, this power is exercised by the study of literature, the literature of Greece and Rome, and especially history. For history broadens and elevates the mind and equips it with a rich store of material. Among the historians, Tacitus was singled out as the first who wrote philosophic history; and in Gibbon's own day the laurels were worn by Hume. It was Hume's conviction that 'the chief use of history is to discover the constant and universal principles of human nature'.[19] It shows us men in all kinds of situations, and it supplies us with the raw material from which we may form our observations. Through the study of history we may become acquainted with 'the regular springs' of human behaviour. 'These records of wars, intrigues, factions, and revolutions', Hume wrote, 'are so many collections of experiments, by which the politician or moral philosopher fixes the principles of his science.'[20] But Gibbon goes farther. The philosophic historian is expected not only to furnish his contemporaries with materials which can be used in forming observations about human action; he should also write history in such a way that the universal principles of human nature are illustrated. His study is the study of cause and effect. 'History is for the philosophic spirit what gambling was for the Marquis de Dangeau. He saw a system, relationships, and an order there, where the others saw only the caprices of fortune.'[21] By studying the laws of causation, the philosophic historian seeks to find beneath the ever-changing flow of human affairs truths about the nature and

[18] *Miscellaneous Works*, iv. 58–59. My translation.

[19] Quoted by C. N. Cochrane, 'The Mind of Edward Gibbon', *University of Toronto Quarterly*, xii (Oct. 1942), 15.

[20] Ibid.

[21] *Miscellaneous Works*, iv. 63. My translation.

destiny of man. In this sense his work is, to use Lord Bolingbroke's pertinent phrase, 'philosophy teaching by examples'.[22]

In 1761 Gibbon began to consider seriously several topics for an historical essay, and in the journal which he kept with some fidelity during these years, we have a detailed record of his plans. His projected study of the expedition of Charles VIII from France into Italy was rejected as too insignificant. In his search for a topic which would bring public applause and private satisfaction, he successively chose and put aside the crusade of Richard I, the barons' wars against John and Henry III, the history of the Black Prince, the lives of Titus and Henry V, the life of Sir Philip Sidney, and that of the Marquis of Montrose. He at last selected Sir Walter Raleigh for his hero; the subject was important, and the materials, he felt, had not yet been properly made use of. He had no plans for working on this immediately, because his duties with the militia denied him the leisure and the opportunity of consulting the numerous books he would need. But he did read the life of Raleigh by Birch, the long article in the General Dictionary, also by Birch, and the second volume of Hume's history, which dealt with the reign of Elizabeth. On 10 August he was recalled to camp, and further work was suspended until January 1762, when, after some study, he felt that his subject was even more appropriate to his aims than he had previously realized.

While he was exploring the Raleigh topic, he read with great interest Bishop Hurd's *Commentary on Horace*, and in February 1762 he wrote a little essay on it. The essay would scarcely deserve our attention if it were not for the fact that Gibbon wrote it at a crucial time in his life. The aspiring historian, eager to get his work under way, but unable to do so because of military duties, has many ideas about the composition of epic and dramatic literature. He challenges the thesis that an epic poem should begin *in medias res*; he discusses the nature of comedy and tragedy; he debates the role of the chorus in classical and contemporary tragedy. But most important for us are his remarks, apropos the subject of imitation, on how Milton developed the plan for *Paradise Lost*. The passage is important because Gibbon's thinking on how Milton chose his topic hints strongly at the way he chose his own.

22 *Letters on the Study and Use of History* (Paris, 1808), p. 41.

When Milton conceived the glorious plan of an English epic, he soon saw the most striking subjects had been taken from him; that Homer had taken all morality for his province, and Virgil exhausted the subject of politics. Religion remained; but as Paganism, though it furnished very agreeable scenes of machinery, took too slight a hold on men's minds to build the story of the epopoea upon it, he had recourse to Christianity; and, taking his story from an article of our faith, struck out a new species of epic poetry; but he could never have done it, had not the manners of that age, attached to religion in general, and to that tenet in particular, warmed his imagination, and given it a dignity and importance, which he could never have transfused into his poem, if he had not first felt it himself. Nor is this observation repugnant to another I have made elsewhere,—that the manners of the ancients were more favorable to poetry than ours. I think so still, of their manners, as well as their languages. Yet I would have our poets employ our own, not only for the sake of variety, but because we shall make the best use of those with which we are the most intimately acquainted.[23]

Three elements in this passage deserve special emphasis: first, Gibbon's recognition that Milton had struck out a new species of epic poetry; second, his understanding of the important relation between the age in which one writes and the nature of the composition; and third, his appreciation of the bearing which the author's conviction has on the finished work of art. In the eighteenth century the epic was considered the noblest form of human art, Aristotle notwithstanding. Dr. Johnson, who may speak for his age on most matters, says: 'By the general consent of criticks, the first praise of genius is due to the writer of an epick poem, as it requires an assemblage of all the powers which are singly sufficient for other compositions.'[24] But the eighteenth century was interested in experimenting with the form and method of the epic, and the English novel is partly the result of such experimentation. Fielding said in the preface to *Joseph Andrews* that he hoped to write a comic epic in prose; *Tom Jones* is in many ways just such an attempt. Gibbon, incidentally a great admirer of Fielding, realizing that the taste of his age as well as his own inclinations attached primary importance to history, might well consider an

[23] *Miscellaneous Works*, iv. 150.

[24] 'Milton', *Johnson: Prose and Poetry*, Mona Wilson, ed. (Cambridge, Mass., 1951), p. 834.

historical epic. It would be a work of prose, formed by the greatness of the theme, the manners and sentiments of the age, and the deep conviction of the author. He would not be imitating Herodotus or Tacitus any more than Milton had imitated Homer and Virgil. Taking for his theme a study congenial to the taste and interest of a philosophic age, his imagination would be warmed by the conviction of that age, and it would lend to his work both dignity and importance. In the fall of Rome, of course, he found an epic theme. Indeed, the seed of a great work on the Roman empire may have been planted in his mind even at this time. Lord Bolingbroke's *Letters on History* had been published in 1755, and it is unthinkable that the young Gibbon had not read them. Perhaps the original suggestion of *The History of the Decline and Fall* is contained in Bolingbroke's lament over the lost books of Livy: 'I should be glad to exchange, if it were possible, what we have of this history for what we have not. Would you not be glad, my lord, to see in one stupendous draught, the whole progress of that government from liberty to servitude? the whole series of causes and effects, apparent and real, public and private? . . . I am sorry to say it, this part of the Roman story would be not only more curious and more authentic than the former, but of more immediate and more important application to the present state of Britain.'[25] It is hard to think of Gibbon reading these lines without being excited by the challenge they contain.

One is all the more struck by the significance of the comments on Milton when he learns that Gibbon returned to his study of Homer just about the time he wrote them, and that he continued with this study throughout the months between February and July. His interest in the nature and the structure of the epic is further shown by two later works: 'An Inquiry whether a Catalogue of the Armies sent into the Field is an essential part of an Epic Poem' (23 December 1763), and 'Critical Observations on the Design of the Sixth Book of the Aeneid' (1770). But it is more important for us to note that sometime between February and July 1762, shortly after his discussion of how Milton selected his topic and while he was deeply involved in a study of Homer, Gibbon decided to change the plans for his history.

In his journal entry for 26 July he abandons the proposed life

[25] pp. 117–18.

of Sir Walter. He found that he could add little to Oldy's work except possibly a better style. Parts of the life are barren of materials. Furthermore, no period of English history has been so thoroughly studied as the reigns of Elizabeth and James I. Beyond this difficulty, the period is fraught with contention and every writer is supposed to take a side. Even though the life of Raleigh is an interesting one, 'his actions are of so subaltern a nature and his writings so confined to the language they were composed in that his fame can hardly ever pass the limits of our island'.[26] To the young man who was searching for a significant topic and European fame, to the man who may already have been thinking in terms of an historical epic, the conclusion was simple; he must find another subject.

> There is one subject I should prefer to all others, it is *The History of the Liberty of the Swiss,* which that brave people recovered from the house of Austria, defended against the Dauphin, afterwards Lewis XI, and at last sealed with the blood of Charles. From such a subject, so full of real virtue, public spirit, military glory, and great lessons of gouvernment, the meanest writer must catch fire. What might not I hope for, who to some talents perhaps add an affection for the nation which would make me labour the composition *con amore.*[27]

An interesting shift in Gibbon's thinking is apparent here. Earlier he had tended to group a historical study around a man. Raleigh was his hero, or Sidney, or Richard I. Now, with a more comprehensive organizing principle he searches for a theme. It is the *liberty* of the Swiss which interests him; the subject is likewise congenial to his own philosophic age, and further, it is one on which he can labour with conviction. But the materials for the study of the Republic of Switzerland were not accessible to him, being largely 'locked up in a barbarous old German language' which he could not bring himself to learn. He continues: 'I have another subject in view, which is the contrast of the former history: the one a poor, warlike, virtuous Republic, which emerges into glory and freedom; the other a Commonwealth, soft, opulent, and corrupt, which, by just degrees, is precipitated from the abuse to the loss of her liberty: both lessons are, perhaps, equally instruc-

[26] *Gibbon's Journal,* D. M. Low, ed. (London, 1929), p. 103.
[27] Ibid.

tive.'[28] The second subject was the history of the Republic of Florence under the house of the Medici, a history which he never wrote. Either of these histories would offer much on which a philosophic historian could exercise his genius. Moreover, both studies had to do with the matter of freedom and liberty. He got so far as to complete the introduction to the Swiss history in 1767, but he abandoned it to work exclusively on *The Decline and Fall.* He seems never to have pursued the second topic, and with good reason; for this dealt with 'a Commonwealth . . . precipitated from the abuse to the loss of her liberty'. These words may be applied not only to Florence; they also describe *The History of the Decline and Fall of the Roman Empire.*

Only thirty-six days after the militia was disbanded, Gibbon left on the Grand Tour. He has devoted the pages in his autobiography which deal with this period to an account of his friends and the social life at Paris and Lausanne. The months which intervened between his arrival at Paris and his visit to Rome were gay and intellectually exciting to a high degree. Gibbon moved among the most fashionable people and the leading literary circles on the Continent. He made the acquaintance of such luminaries of the Enlightenment as d'Alembert and Diderot, d'Holbach and Helvétius, as well as many scholars whose special fields were Greek and Roman history. At the same time he pursued his studies with considerable diligence. In his 'Extraits raisonnés de mes lectures', and in his *Journal,* he describes his reading during this period. What has already been said about Homer is confirmed by entries which indicate that from 27 March to 16 August 1762, he applied himself almost daily to the *Iliad* until he had completed it. This study was accompanied by much collateral reading, such as M. Guichardt's *Mémoires militaires sur les Grecs et sur les Romains,* and occasional rereading of the *Aeneid* for purposes of comparison. On 6 June he records the plan of giving 'part of my day to Homer and part to Quintilian; that is, to unite the example with the precept'.[29] Homer was followed by a careful study of Longinus and Burke on the sublime (September–November 1762).

[28] In his *Journal,* p. 104, Gibbon wrote: '. . . which by degrees, loses its independency and sinks into the arms of a master'. I have used the later, more elegant language of the *Autobiographies,* p. 197.

[29] *Miscellaneous Works,* v. 224.

There is a hiatus in his records between December 1762 and August 1763, but when we next see Gibbon at work, in Lausanne, he has undertaken all the satires of Juvenal. One comment in particular, on the tenth satire, deserves our notice:

> We perceive throughout, not only the dignity of a true censor, who arraigns vice, exposes folly, and appals guilt, but the soul of a republican, reluctantly bending under the new constitution, the sworn enemy of tyranny, and the friend of a mild and equitable monarchy rather through necessity than inclination. This love of liberty, and loftiness of mind, distinguishes Juvenal from all the poets who lived after the establishment of the monarchy. Virgil, Horace, Ovid, Lucan, Martial, Statius, Valerius, Flaccus, all sing the ruin of their country, and the triumph of its oppressors.[30]

The republican sentiments, the love of liberty, and the loftiness of mind which Gibbon saw in Juvenal were congenial to his own spirit, and they helped form his understanding of the role played by Augustus in the ruin of the empire.

Between 7 September and 3 December 1763 Gibbon was occupied with a daily and very close study of two important works on ancient Italy. He read the description of ancient Rome by Fabiano Nardini, and Cluverius's *Italia antiqua.* These he selected to prepare him for the forthcoming journey to Italy and to assist him in his future studies. He had been forming a 'geographical collection of Italy' and hoped that his journey would augment it, so that on his return to England he might write a description of ancient Italy which would be the joint result of his studies, his reflections, and his observations. By 30 December he was able to record that there remained nothing for him to read on this subject except the books by Strabo; and after completing these he undertook Ovid's *Fasti* and Spanheim's *De Praestantia et usu numismatum,* proposing to add the study of medals and antiquities to that of geography. By the end of February and throughout March 1764 he was at work completing the drafts of his Geography, which has come down to us as *Nomina gentesque antiquae Italiae.* Not many young Englishmen were so thoroughly prepared for the Italian part of the Grand Tour!

In April he left Lausanne. We find him in Genoa in early June,

[30] *Miscellaneous Works,* v. 297.

and through the hot summer months he studied Italian and the arts in the agreeable city of Florence. It was not until October that he finally reached Rome. The unaffected diction of the letter which he wrote his father after his arrival expresses his sentiments more eloquently, perhaps, than the polished and deliberate prose of the autobiography.

I am now, Dear Sir, at Rome. If it was difficult before to give you or Mrs. Gibbon any account of what I saw, it is impossible here. I have already found such a fund of entertainment for a mind somewhat prepared for it by an acquaintance with the Romans, that I am really almost in a dream. Whatever ideas books may have given us of the greatness of that people, their accounts of the most flourishing state of Rome fall infinitely short of the picture of its ruins.[31]

The modern student, fortunately, is able to gain some knowledge of what Rome must have looked like about the time Gibbon first saw it. The drawings of Piranesi (1720–78) have preserved for us numerous glimpses of the Capitol. Although allowances surely must be made for the artistic sensibilities of different personalities, these engravings appear to have been conceived in something of the spirit with which Gibbon first looked on the ruins. Modern archaeology has done much to remove the dirt and rubble from around the great columns and scattered members of the temples and other buildings of antiquity. In Rome today the spacious porticoes of the palaces and the monuments of the Caesars are carefully preserved as museum pieces. But in Gibbon's day swine and buffalo might be seen grazing in the Forum. The columns of the great pillars were almost buried, and their enormous Corinthian capitals from sheer size and beauty of workmanship insulted the degenerate Italians who played dice in their shadows. Garbage, rubble, and filth added to the contrast of present decay and past greatness.

Looking back on this experience from the distance of twenty-five years, Gibbon wrote:

I can neither forget nor express the strong emotions which agitated my mind as I first approached and entered the *eternal City*. After a sleepless night, I trod with lofty step the ruins of the Forum; each

[31] *The Letters of Edward Gibbon*, J. E. Norton, ed. (3 vols., New York, 1956), i. 184.

memorable spot where Romulus *stood*, or Tully spoke, or Caesar fell was at once present to my eye; and several days of intoxication were lost or enjoyed before I could descend to a cool and minute investigation.[32]

If 'The Gibbon' (as he calls himself in letters to Sheffield) ever felt a surge of true enthusiasm, it was probably at this time. In his letter to his father he had modestly referred to his prior acquaintance with the Romans. The man who had read all of Latin literature and had sought to imbibe from it a spirit most congenial to his own, the writer who had prepared himself for this moment by exhausting all the materials on the geography of ancient Italy, surely had reached his spiritual home. When we reflect on Gibbon's development, it comes as no surprise that during this visit the aspiring historian hit upon the idea of writing a history of the decline and fall of the city. As the subject expanded in his mind, its magnitude must have induced him to hesitate for a considerable time before undertaking it. The fact that he continued to entertain the history of the Swiss as a possible topic and even wrote an introduction to it suggests that he wanted to try out his powers on a middle flight before attempting his magnum opus; but there can be little doubt that from the time of this visit to Rome, all the powers and aspirations of Edward Gibbon began to point towards a great history of the Roman empire. Here was a topic which offered the highest challenge to a philosophic historian. Like Milton, Gibbon had dedicated himself at an early age to the execution of some great work. His studies had been directed to the discovery of a suitable topic. Twelve years were to intervene between this initial plan for a history of the city and the publication of the first volume of *The Decline and Fall*, but they were years in which the young scholar, with a new sense of direction and purpose, worked with increasing intensity on Roman history. His close study of the epic, his preoccupation with freedom, his spiritual affinity with Republican and Imperial Rome, each played a part in his selection of his topic; and emulation of his great contemporaries and of the most distinguished classical writers drove him forward on his gigantic, self-appointed task.

The plan of his history and the skill with which it is executed

[32] *Autobiographies*, p. 267.

will be examined by an internal study of the work itself; but before we turn to *The Decline and Fall* I should touch upon Gibbon's selection of English as the linguistic vehicle for his great work. As a citizen of Europe, seeking international recognition, Gibbon might well have chosen French as his literary language. His first published work was in French, and as late as 1767, when he had already done some work on the fall of Rome, he was writing history in that language: his *Introduction à l'histoire générale de la République des Suisses*. But his friend Georges Deyverdun had shown David Hume the manuscript of this essay, and in a letter dated 24 October 1767, Hume wrote Gibbon that he had read the introduction to the Swiss history with pleasure. He added,

> I have only one objection, derived from the language in which it is written. Why do you compose in French, and carry faggots into the wood, as Horace says with regard to Romans who wrote in Greek? I grant that you have a like motive to those Romans, and adopt a language much more generally diffused than your native tongue: but have you not remarked the fate of those two ancient languages in the following ages? The Latin, though then less celebrated, and confined to more narrow limits, has in some measure outlived the Greek, and is now more generally understood by men of letters. Let the French, therefore, triumph in the present diffusion of their tongue. Our solid and increasing establishments in America, where we need less dread the inundation of Barbarians, promise a superior stability and duration to the English language.[33]

Gibbon's admiration for Hume was considerable, and this letter made a deep impression on him. Earlier, in planning his essay on the study of literature, he admitted that he wrote in French not only because it was the familiar language of his conversation and studies, but also because he wished to be generally understood on the Continent. The problem is an old one for European writers. They desire, on the one hand, the greatest dissemination of their works. On the other hand, they are motivated by a spirit of patriotism to use their own language. Milton addressed civilized Europe in Latin, but chose his native tongue for his noblest efforts. Leibnitz and Frederick the Great used French. Temperament and taste also play a role in the selection of language, and Hume appealed to Gibbon's judgement on these matters also: 'Your use

[33] *Autobiographies*, p. 277, n.

of the French tongue has also led you into a style more poetical and figurative, and more highly coloured, than our language seems to admit of in historical productions. . . .'[34] These were the words of the master, and they were enough to convince Gibbon that he should use English. The lasting impression Hume's letter made on Gibbon is attested to by a comment he wrote some years later at the end of the thirty-eighth chapter of *The Decline and Fall.* He takes comfort in the thought that the flourishing colonies in America offer European civilization a secure refuge against any future barbarian invasions; and in a footnote he adds, 'we may reflect with some pleasure that the English language will probably be diffused over an immense and populous continent'.[35] As an interesting example of the fulfilment of Gibbon's hopes, we can record that the young Abraham Lincoln, just before he entered politics, read with keen interest a volume of *The Decline and Fall of the Roman Empire.*

[34] *Autobiographies*, p. 277, n.

[35] *The Decline and Fall*, iv. 166, n. 8. I am indebted to Professor Arnold Toynbee for much of this discussion of linguistic vehicle, especially the comment about Abraham Lincoln. See *A Study of History* (5 vols., London, 1939), v. 643–5.

II · THE ARGUMENT

> Reason is free, and Reason he made right,
> But bid her well be ware, and still erect,
> Lest by some fair appearing good surprised
> She dictate false, and misinform the will. . . .
> *Paradise Lost*, ix. 352–5

WHEN Gibbon was half-way through the composition of *The Decline and Fall*, he wrote to his friend Lord Sheffield: 'I am building a great book, which, besides the three stories already exposed to the public eye, will have three stories more before we reach the roof and battlements.'[1] The comparison of his work to architecture will strike his readers as just, for *The Decline and Fall* does give the appearance of being a solidly constructed edifice, with a unity of design and harmony of proportion in all the parts. Peter Quennell has remarked that 'there is probably no book of equal size and scope more thoroughly imbued with the characteristic quality of a single man's intelligence'.[2] To this statement may be added another: the entire structure is unified by a single theme which Gibbon never changes and which lies in what may be called 'the creative centre' of the work. Even the style shows only slight modification and variation as the work progresses. Throughout the whole there is evident a single complex attitude which is applied to the management of every part. But, as J. Middleton Murry has said: 'Great work simply will not yield up its full significance, its essential beauty, at the first reading; not until you have patiently worked your way into the creative centre can you truly say that you apprehend it; and only when you have truly apprehended a work of literature are you in a position to make positive declarations about its style.'[3] In this chapter I shall try to define some of the essential elements which are found at the creative

[1] *The Letters of Edward Gibbon*, J. E. Norton, ed. (3 vols., New York, 1956), iii. 59.

[2] *The Profane Virtues* (New York, 1945), p. 98.

[3] *The Problem of Style* (London, 1922), p. 35.

centre in the hope that a knowledge of them will assist us in appreciating what Gibbon has done in the whole work.

On 27 June 1787 Gibbon completed the last lines of *The Decline and Fall*. For him at that moment, as at the beginning of his study, the history of the destruction of the empire of Rome was 'the greatest, perhaps, and most awful scene in the history of mankind'.[4] The long narrative covers almost fourteen centuries of the history of Western civilization, centuries which witnessed the agonizing transition from ancient to modern greatness. The most obvious organizing principle was the fate of Rome, and all events connected with this story had to be included. Starting with the empire at the beginning of the second century after Christ, the age of the Antonines, the narrative moves forward, taking up the emperors, the battles, and all those thousands of persons and events of the tortured millennium which eventually gave birth to the modern world. The history takes us as far east as the great wall of China, and even to Korea; as far south as the land of Abyssinia; as far north as England, Norway, and even Lapland; as far west as the pillars of Hercules. Many of the great figures of the world parade through Gibbon's pages: Constantine, Justinian, Saint Augustine and Boethius, Julian and Belisarius, Genghis Khan and Tamburlaine, Alaric and Attila, Athanasius and Chrysostom. The manners, morals, and economies of the Roman empire and of all those empires and nations which participated in her destruction find their logical places in the fascinating tale. The migrations of the Goths, Huns, Vandals, and Alemanni, the empires of the Byzantines, Franks, Persians, Arabs, Mongols, and Turks constitute some of the rich material which bears directly on the main theme. The fall of Rome was accelerated by the shock of religious conflict, and the history includes the rise and, Gibbon would say, the fall of two of the world's greatest religions, Mohammedanism and Christianity, along with a survey of the final destruction of paganism. In the gigantic migrations of the period we see the conflict of continents, the stirring tales of the crusades and the Turkish-European struggles. These narratives are further illustrated by careful inquiries into special subjects which bear closely on the main drama. In one chapter (XLIV), for example,

[4] *The History of the Decline and Fall of the Roman Empire*, J. B. Bury, ed. (7 vols., London, 1896–1900), vii. 325.

Gibbon pauses to examine 1,000 years of Roman jurisprudence; in another he studies the manners and customs of pastoral nations. In this tremendous spectacle of the rise and fall of civilizations, almost every human passion and action is involved. There is no virtue or vice that cannot be found in the pages of Gibbon. *The Decline and Fall* is one of the greatest pictures of the struggles of humanity to manage its own affairs for its own interest and progress; in short, the great history is a picture of human life itself, drawn from one particular point of view.

As David Hume might have observed, the scope of *The Decline and Fall* offered ample room for the philosophic historian to discover the constant and universal principles of human nature. And for the writer seeking literary fame, the epic size of the history provided the utmost range for all his powers. Milton had aspired to make apparent to men the justice of God's ways; Gibbon, writing as a philosophic sceptic, sought to illustrate by a study of fourteen centuries of human history, a great secular truth for mankind. The mention of philosophic scepticism, however, suggests that before inquiring into Gibbon's theme we consider briefly one of the deliberately imposed limitations of the history.

A Hebrew prophet will see in the calamities visited upon his kingdom the punishment of God: the Assyrian horde is simply the rod of God's anger. Virgil found divine sanction for the civilizing mission of Rome. Milton interpreted the history of the world since Adam in terms of man's first disobedience, or, as Gibbon put it, selected an article of faith on which to base his epic. But Gibbon carefully and deliberately excludes from his study of human history any and all influence of Providence and the operation of the supernatural. Prophecy, revelation, divine sanction, and the marvellous are dismissed as beyond the scope of rational inquiry; and Gibbon quotes the sentiments of Procopius with obvious approval: '"that religious controversy is the offspring of arrogance and folly; that true piety is most laudably expressed by silence and submission; that man, ignorant of his own nature, should not presume to scrutinize the nature of his God; and that it is sufficient for us to know that power and benevolence are the perfect attributes of the Deity"'.[5] The philosophic historian is

[5] v. 133.

interested in discovering the natural laws of man and society. As Pope said, a number of years before Gibbon wrote:

> Know then thyself, presume not God to scan;
> The proper study of mankind is man.

There are many places in *The Decline and Fall* where Gibbon runs up against the limitations of human reason, and he always stops at the boundary line between what is for him light and shade. His comment on the Koran is characteristic: 'The communication of ideas requires a similitude of thought and language; the discourse of a philosopher would vibrate, without effect, on the ear of a peasant; yet how minute is the distance of *their* understandings if it be compared with the contact of an infinite and a finite mind, with the word of God expressed by the tongue or the pen of a mortal? . . . If the composition of the Koran exceed the faculties of a man, to what superior intelligence should we ascribe the Iliad of Homer or the Philippics of Demosthenes?'[6] He holds back not only from works supposed to be revelations or to have been divinely inspired, but also from 'the fleeting shadows of metaphysics'. Often enough he enjoys a witty thrust at the expense of those who will chart 'the infinite void', and his own restraint is the source of some of his most effective irony. Where reason cannot penetrate, he turns away, content to seek natural causes for events.

From a purely literary point of view such rationalism may seem overriding to some readers, and to them it may appear as the source of a real limitation in the artistic enjoyment of *The Decline and Fall.* They will point out that much of the power of the greatest literature stems from an awareness of the existence of what is more than man. The merciless chain of events in *Oedipus Rex,* or the great purposiveness of the *Aeneid,* the cosmic rebellion of Satan in *Paradise Lost,* and the frightful power of evil in *Lear,* will come to mind to illustrate the extra dimension to be achieved by serious reflection on the question of man's relation to the unknown. Gibbon dismisses such reflections from *The Decline and Fall*; yet the exclusion is none the less the source of different kinds of strength. He never denies the ultimate mystery of human existence, but he asserts the dignity and importance of man in the

[6] v. 342–3.

face of the mystery and seeks the amelioration of human life through a development of purely human faculties. The courage of his assertion is all the greater because of the fact that he believes that man cannot know. *The Decline and Fall* is acted out in front of a black curtain, with our attention fixed on the actors. The actors, however, are often lost, wandering, and degenerate, and their very crimes and follies remind us of the outer blackness which surrounds the spectacle. The tremendous pageant is placed in 'the boundless annals of time', and the melancholy which overlies the entire work, although always disciplined and controlled, is intensified as succeeding generations pass down into the grave. Such details as the moving lines of Persian poetry which Mohammed II is said to have quoted on the capture of Constantinople remind the reader that, however clear the spectacle itself may be, its ultimate meaning rests in the unknown.

> The spider has wove his web in the imperial palace; and the owl hath sung her watch-song on the towers of Afrasiab.[7]

Moreover, the clarity of the spectacle is a virtue. The limits between light and darkness are carefully drawn; and, compelled to find reasonable explanations for the actions of men and the fall of empires, Gibbon tries to bring all of his material into the daylight area of the mind. Dusty objects, buried under centuries of superstition, myth, or fable, are suddenly illuminated with an astonishing clarity; and, if one wishes to debate with Gibbon on the merit of his interpretation, he must either meet him in the same broad daylight where the interpretation was originally made or challenge the validity of his imposing such limitations on his inquiry. The philosophic historian aimed to discover natural and primary, as well as immediate causes in the great pageant of human affairs; and, when his investigations fail, he confesses his ignorance to his reader. We should note in passing that even the sense of nemesis which is operative in the background is explained in purely natural terms.

I should now like to consider why, in Gibbon's opinion, Rome fell; or to put it another way, what rational meaning he found in this awful spectacle. The inquiry will anticipate a somewhat fuller explanation of the 'argument' of *The Decline and Fall*, so I may

[7] vii. 199.

simplify a complex picture. There is a core idea around which the many specific and secondary causes group themselves. Stated in its simplest form, it is that the Romans, for a variety of reasons, were content to abdicate the responsibilities of freedom. Blinded by the comforts of a specious prosperity, they first abused and then lost their freedom. Rome decayed internally before it was possible for the barbarians to triumph over her. Indeed, Gibbon points out that Rome would have fallen even if there had been no barbarians to make the conquest. The too frequently quoted remark, 'I have described the triumph of barbarism and religion', by being removed from context, has blurred the fact that in Gibbon's view neither could have triumphed had not the Romans abandoned strenuous liberty for temporary prosperity. 'If all the Barbarian conquerors had been annihilated in the same hour, their total destruction would not have restored the empire of the West', he says on one occasion, 'and if Rome still survived, she survived the loss of freedom, of virtue, and of honour.'[8]

In the first three chapters Gibbon presents a magnificent survey of the Roman world in the age of the Antonines. Of this period, one passage in particular has been mistakenly quoted by several writers as embodying Gibbon's ideal of government. He wrote:

> If a man were called to fix the period in the history of the world during which the condition of the human race was most happy and prosperous, he would, without hesitation, name that which elapsed from the death of Domitian to the accession of Commodus. The vast extent of the Roman empire was governed by absolute power, under the guidance of virtue and wisdom. The armies were restrained by the firm but gentle hand of four successive emperors, whose characters and authority commanded involuntary respect. The forms of the civil administration were carefully preserved by Nerva, Trajan, Hadrian, and the Antonines, who delighted in the image of liberty, and were pleased with considering themselves as the accountable ministers of the laws. Such princes deserved the honour of restoring the republic, had the Romans of their days been capable of enjoying a rational freedom.[9]

But the Romans of that age were not capable of such enjoyment, Gibbon continues, and this is a point which has not often enough been noticed. After speaking of the exquisite delight of beholding

[8] iii. 480. [9] i. 78.

the general happiness of which these emperors were the authors, he writes: 'A just but melancholy reflection embittered, however, the noblest of human enjoyments. They must often have recollected the instability of a happiness which depended on the character of a single man.'[10] The Romans permitted Augustus absolute power, and he subverted the constitution; or, as Gibbon expresses the idea in a later passage, 'it was artfully contrived by Augustus that, in the enjoyment of plenty, the Romans should lose the memory of freedom'.[11] Gibbon had previously described the government instituted by Augustus in one concise passage: 'it may be defined an absolute monarchy disguised by the forms of a commonwealth. The masters of the Roman world surrounded their throne with darkness, concealed their irresistible strength, and humbly professed themselves the accountable ministers of the senate, whose supreme decrees they dictated and obeyed.'[12]

Much later in the work, when Gibbon has come to the reign of the feeble son of Theodosius, the Emperor Honorius, he pauses to consider how the impending fall of the Roman empire might have been avoided. He has mentioned the intention of Honorius of convening an annual assembly of the seven provinces of Gaul. This assembly was to consist of the governors, the magistrates of the cities, and perhaps the bishops, along with a number of the landowners, and it was to have considerable power. Gibbon continues:

If such an institution, which gave the people an interest in their own government, had been universally established by Trajan or the Antonines, the seeds of public wisdom and virtue might have been cherished and propagated in the empire of Rome. The privileges of the subject would have secured the throne of the monarch; the abuses of an arbitrary administration might have been prevented, in some degree, or corrected, by the interposition of these representative assemblies; and the country would have been defended against a foreign enemy by the arms of natives and freemen. *Under the mild and generous influence of liberty, the Roman empire might have remained invincible and immortal*; or, if its excessive magnitude and the instability of human affairs had opposed such perpetual continuance, its vital and constituent members might have separately preserved their vigour and independence.[13]

[10] i. 78. [11] ii. 156. [12] i. 68.
[13] iii. 357. Italics mine.

But Trajan and the Antonines instituted no such plan of constitutional liberty, and the three-chapter survey of the Roman world under their reigns, far from illustrating Gibbon's concept of the ideal in human affairs, is deeply coloured by signs of imminent and inevitable decay. Indeed, like the authors of epic poetry who follow the convention of stating their theme in the opening lines of the verse, Gibbon states the theme of *The Decline and Fall* in this introductory survey. The armies, no longer activated by patriotism, which, he points out, 'is derived from a strong sense of our own interest in the preservation and prosperity of the free government of which we are members',[14] were inspired to battle by the skilful arts of the emperors. The arts and sciences ceased to flourish. 'The beauties of the poets and orators, instead of kindling a fire like their own, inspired only cold and servile imitations. . . . A cloud of critics, of compilers, of commentators, darkened the face of learning, and the decline of genius was soon followed by the corruption of taste.'[15] Instead of resulting in health and prosperity, the 'long peace, and the uniform government of the Romans, introduced a slow and secret poison into the vitals of the empire. The minds of men were gradually reduced to the same level, the fire of genius was extinguished, and even the military spirit evaporated.'[16]

Gibbon's remarks concerning the melancholy reflection of the Antonines, that the happiness of which they were the authors depended on the character of a single man, are followed by the further point that these gloomy apprehensions had already been justified by the history of tyranny. The golden age of Trajan and the Antonines had been preceded by an age of iron, he writes, and Tiberius, Caligula, Claudius, Nero, Vitellius, and Domitian earn the epithet 'monsters'. He concludes his survey by giving the reasons why the slavery of the Romans under the tyrants who preceded the Antonines 'was more wretched than that of the victims of tyranny in any other age or country', and the three-chapter study of Roman prosperity ends on the ominous remark: '"Wherever you are," said Cicero to the exiled Marcellus, "remember that you are equally within the power of the conqueror."'[17]

The age of the Antonines may have been the happiest in the

[14] i. 10. [15] i. 57–58. [16] i. 56. [17] i. 82.

history of man, but Gibbon asserts that 'all that is human must retrograde if it do not advance',[18] and, man's nature being what it is, this period with its specious prosperity was inevitably brief. Benevolent despotism remains benevolent at the will of the despot, and uniformity produces sterility. Against such a picture, indeed, while he is drawing it, Gibbon poses his political ideal: 'A martial nobility and stubborn commons, possessed of arms, tenacious of property, and collected into constitutional assemblies, form the only balance capable of preserving a free constitution against the enterprises of an aspiring prince.'[19] Much later in the work, when his picture of the fall of the empire in the west is completed and he has developed the slavery of Byzantium, Gibbon becomes very explicit about what his narrative has indicated thus far. The sterility which results from tyranny of the state and of the spirit is opposed by Gibbon's views of strenuous, competitive liberty.

> In all the pursuits of active and speculative life, the emulation of states and individuals is the most powerful spring of the efforts and improvements of mankind. The cities of ancient Greece were cast in the happy mixture of union and independence, which is repeated on a larger scale, but in a looser form, by the nations of modern Europe: the union of language, religion, and manners, which renders them the spectators and judges of each other's merit; the independence of government and interest, which asserts their separate freedom, and excites them to strive for pre-eminence in the career of glory. The situation of the Romans was less favourable; yet in the early ages of the republic, which fixed the national character, a similar emulation was kindled among the states of Latium and Italy; and in the arts and sciences, they aspired to equal or surpass their Grecian masters. *The empire of the Caesars undoubtedly checked the activity and progress of the human mind. . . .*[20]

Such efforts for the improvement of mankind exist only under the conditions of freedom, Gibbon says, and as the philosophic historian discusses emulation as the most powerful spring for the betterment of life, we are getting closer to the centre of *The Decline and Fall.*

As for the individual, the first step towards freedom is a liberating education, especially a study of the great classics of Greece and

[18] vii. 304. [19] i. 59. [20] vi. 108–9. Italics mine.

Rome. This point is illustrated in many passages, but one of the most explicit statements is found in a discussion of the learning of the Mohammedans: 'the classics have much to teach. . . . The philosophers of Athens and Rome enjoyed the blessings, and asserted the rights, of civil and religious freedom. Their moral and political writings might have gradually unlocked the fetters of Eastern Despotism, diffused a liberal spirit of enquiry and toleration, and encouraged the Arabian sages to suspect that their caliph was a tyrant and their prophet an impostor.'[21]

We are now moving into a position where Gibbon's antagonism to Christianity and his complete lack of sympathy for the Byzantine empire are more intelligible. On the matter of Christian institutions his views are rather bluntly expressed in one passage on the institution of monasticism: 'The freedom of the mind, the source of every generous and rational sentiment, was destroyed by the habits of credulity and submission; and the monk, contracting the vices of a slave, devoutly followed the faith and passions of his ecclesiastical tyrant.'[22] As for Byzantium, Gibbon's contempt for a servile and enervated people is well summed up in his description of the thousands of parasites who gorged themselves on the luxury surrounding the throne: 'Their honours and emoluments, their dress and titles, their mutual salutations and respective pre-eminence, were balanced with more exquisite labour than would have fixed the constitution of a free people; and the code was almost perfect when this baseless fabric, the monument of pride and servitude, was forever buried in the ruins of the empire.'[23]

The freedom of the mind is the source of every generous and rational sentiment—this thought brings us to the creative centre of *The Decline and Fall,* where the emotions, attitudes, values, and principles, indistinguishable from each other, act together to form the style in which all the parts of the work are executed. On the one hand there is the mass of irreducible factual information which the historian cannot distort and still claim to be an historian. On the other, there is the free spirit of the artist playing over his material, shaping it and commenting upon it. The spirit is that of an urbane, sophisticated sceptic. What Gibbon says of the education of the Romans under the early empire might have

[21] vi. 33. [22] iv. 66. [23] vi. 83.

been applied to himself: 'The education of Helvidius and Thrasea, of Tacitus and Pliny, was the same as that of Cato and Cicero. From Grecian philosophy they had imbibed the justest and most liberal notions of the dignity of human nature and the origin of civil society. The history of their own country had taught them to revere a free, a virtuous, and a victorious commonwealth; to abhor the successful crimes of Caesar and Augustus. . . .'[24] Gibbon held as the fundamental conviction of his life and work that man could fulfil his destiny only under conditions of spiritual and political freedom. In his *Autobiography*, after he had completed *The Decline and Fall*, he wrote: 'Freedom is the first wish of our heart; freedom is the first blessing of our nature; and, unless we bind ourselves with the voluntary chains of interest or passion, we advance in freedom as we advance in years.'[25] This is the spirit, then, which transforms a mere mass of learning into a great humanistic achievement, and the firm anchor of his humanism rests securely in Greco-Roman literature.

Just as Gibbon has given us a statement of his ideal in respect to government, and strenuous, competitive liberty, so we find in an early part of *The Decline and Fall* a full statement of his ideal in respect to human nature. This occurs in a discussion of the origins and growth of Christianity, and is used by Gibbon to set in perspective the other-worldly aspirations of the Christians.

There are two very natural propensities which we may distinguish in the most virtuous and liberal dispositions, the love of pleasure and the love of action. If the former be refined by art and learning, improved by the charms of social intercourse, and corrected by a just regard to economy, to health, and to reputation, it is productive of the greatest part of the happiness of private life. The love of action is a principle of a much stronger and more doubtful nature. It often leads to anger, to ambition, and to revenge; but when it is guided by the sense of propriety and benevolence, it becomes the parent of every virtue; and, if those virtues are accompanied with equal abilities, a family, a state, or an empire, may be indebted for their safety and prosperity to the undaunted courage of a single man. To the love of pleasure we may therefore ascribe most of the agreeable, to the love of action we may attribute most of the useful and respectable quali-

[24] i. 80.

[25] *The Autobiographies of Edward Gibbon*, John Murray, ed. (London, 1896), p. 61.

fications. The character in which both the one and the other should be united and harmonized would seem to constitute the most perfect idea of human nature. The insensible and inactive disposition, which should be supposed alike destitute of both, would be rejected, by the common consent of mankind, as utterly incapable of procuring any happiness to the individual, or any public benefit to the world. But it was not in *this* world that the primitive Christians were desirous of making themselves either agreeable or useful.[26]

The reader will have noticed under the carefully draped folds of the Roman toga the sudden flash of steel which emerges from the last sentence, and it is clearly in this world that Gibbon found the proper sphere for human fulfilment.

Here we might recall Gibbon's remark on his reading of Cicero: 'I breathed the spirit of freedom, and I imbibed from his precepts and examples the public and private sense of a man.'[27] There is a close parallel between Gibbon's portrait of the perfection of human nature and the standards set forth in Cicero's *De Officiis*. This work, as is commonly known, is a kind of summary of the moral principles of classical humanism. Its content has been well described by a modern scholar, C. N. Cochrane:

> In this essay the author gives final utterance to his conviction that the end for which nature has designed mankind is the achievement of what may be called empirical self-hood, and that the purpose of organized society is to promote its development by establishing and maintaining adequate social controls. In so doing, Cicero proclaims an ideal of excellence not unworthy of human beings. At the same time, he insists upon their capacity to realize that ideal through a self-imposed discipline in which the passions are subjected to the control of reason; and in this he sees a possibility of transcending the limitations of barbarism and of 'civilizing' without suppressing the ego.[28]

The achievement of man's destiny, for Gibbon as for Cicero, meant perfecting human nature; and the value of organized society is judged according to the extent to which it does or does not provide a proper context within which such achievement is possible. The oppression of tyranny, at one extreme, and the

[26] ii. 34–35.

[27] *The Memoirs of the Life of Edward Gibbon*, George B. Hill, ed. (New York, 1900), p. 92.

[28] *Christianity and Classical Culture* (Oxford, 1940), pp. 56–57.

anarchy of perfect equality at the other, are detrimental to the maximum extent to this purpose. Individual perfection was approached as men subdued their overriding passions and submitted themselves to the guidance of 'right reason'. The collective destiny of man was realized in his civilizing of himself and his fellows.

That these sentiments are central to *The Decline and Fall* may be illustrated by numerous passages. Gibbon's discussion of Cicero's concept of 'right reason' is found in the chapter on Roman jurisprudence, and it is interesting to note that he comes closer here to entertaining seriously a philosophical mystery than in any other place in the history. Cicero, says Gibbon, 'labours to deduce from a celestial origin the wisdom and justice of the Roman constitution. The whole universe, according to his sublime hypothesis, forms one immense commonwealth; gods and men, who participate of the same essence, are members of the same community; reason prescribes the law of nature and nations; and all positive institutions, however modified by accident or custom, are drawn from the rule of right, which the Deity has inscribed on every virtuous mind.'[29] As for the rule of right, Gibbon seems to be thinking of this when he writes: 'Yet the Hungarians were not devoid of those principles of justice and humanity which nature has implanted in every bosom. . . . Among the barbarians, there were many whose spontaneous virtue supplied their laws and corrected their manners. . . .'[30] In Gibbon's view the essence of civilization consists in the control of passions and instincts by the law of nature and nations which reason has prescribed. Indeed, he goes so far as to say that 'the different characteristics which distinguish the civilized nations of the globe may be ascribed to the use and the abuse of reason',[31] and reason, he insists, can function only under conditions of liberty.

A further illustration of how deeply imbedded in Gibbon's thinking these views are is found in his discussion of the passive obedience of the early Christians: 'The Protestants of France, of Germany, and of Britain, who asserted with such intrepid courage their civil and religious freedom, have been insulted by the invidious comparison between the conduct of the primitive and of the reformed Christians. Perhaps, instead of censure, some applause may be due to the superior sense and spirit of our

[29] iv. 457. [30] vi. 141–2. [31] iii. 71.

ancestors who had convinced themselves that religion cannot abolish the unalienable rights of human nature.'[32] Among the unalienable rights of human nature, Gibbon would place freedom of the conscience and of the mind. Such freedom is the first step to curiosity and knowledge;[33] it is the first step towards the improvement of man. More than once in *The Decline and Fall*, when authentic historical materials are scarce, Gibbon is able to conjecture on the basis of his 'knowledge of human nature, and of the sure operations of its fierce and unrestrained passions'.[34] When these passions are released from the control of the reason, or when its discipline is in any way impaired, we see that man has little claim to call himself a civilized creature: 'In the fall and the sack of great cities, an historian is condemned to repeat the tale of uniform calamity; and the same effects must be produced by the same passions; and, when those passions may be indulged without control, small, alas! is the difference between civilized and savage man.'[35]

The operation of instinct and unleashed passions is fierce and terrible; but Gibbon affirms his conviction that these passions can be controlled, and even goes so far as to say that the best worship of the Deity is the cultivation of human reason and the development of its powers. His continued interest, throughout the long history, in liberal education, which is a freeing of the mind from the tyranny of instinct, passion, and superstition, is a testament to his faith that men can, without divine aid, on the strength of their own powers, civilize themselves. This is the great aim of individual and social life, and the highest virtue is to be found in the man who contributes to the civilization of his country and his world. For Gibbon the service of mankind in this respect is the best service of God.[36]

The Ciceronian concept of 'right reason' is a commonplace in English humanism, but one usually finds it fused with elements of Christian doctrine, as in the writings of More, Spenser, Hooker, or Milton. In *Paradise Lost*, for example, Milton states that God endowed Adam with 'right reason' before the fall.

[32] ii. 295.

[33] vii. 116.

[34] i. 237.

[35] vii. 197.

[36] He seems to quote Abulpharagius with approval: 'That they are the elect of God, . . . whose lives are devoted to the improvement of their rational faculties.' *The Decline and Fall*, vi. 27.

> But God left free the will, for what obeys
> Reason is free, and Reason he made right. . . . (ix. 351–2)

Adam sins by failing to listen to the dictates of his reason when he places his love for Eve above his love for God. With the fall, the Christian humanists contended, the reason of man was darkened and no longer capable of discovering truth unassisted. Therefore, they argued, God has seen fit to grant man revelation. Their view is rejected by Gibbon implicitly. Nowhere in his pages is there any evidence that he accepted the theological doctrine of original sin, and there is ample evidence that he did not. It is also true that Gibbon implicitly rejects the concept of divine revelation, which he considers with some of his most corrosive irony. The revolution of seventeen centuries, he dryly observes, has instructed us not to press too closely the mysterious language of prophecy and revelation. As for the Mosaic history of the world, Gibbon attempts to dispose of it as energetically as possible in his fifteenth chapter. On the matter of rewards and punishments in after life for conduct on this earth, he stands with Cicero: 'At the bar and in the senate of Rome the ablest orators were not apprehensive of giving offense to their hearers by exposing that doctrine as an idle and extravagant opinion, which was rejected with contempt by every man of a liberal education and understanding.'[37] As for the Christian visions of the New Jerusalem or heavenly city on earth, Gibbon writes them off as a kind of puerile wish-fulfilment. It is not in a heavenly city of this world or of another world that Gibbon and Cicero sought the fulfilment of human destiny, but rather in a city of man. It was against this Roman concept that Saint Augustine erected his idea of *The City of God*, a work which Gibbon read, but an idea which he never accepted.

Like Cicero, Gibbon has a practical cast to his thinking. The pursuit of wisdom as an end in itself yields to the acceptance of public responsibility. Cicero had said, 'To be drawn by study away from active life is contrary to moral duty. For the whole glory of virtue is in activity.'[38] This remark will elucidate many judgements Gibbon makes on the relative merits of the active and speculative life. The reader of *The Decline and Fall* will remember

[37] ii. 20.

[38] Walter Miller (trans.), Cicero, *De Officiis* (Loeb Classical Library [New York, 1913]), i. 6, 19.

Gibbon's contempt for the emperors who indulged themselves in theological disputation while their provinces decayed or were conquered by the barbarians. The high esteem in which he holds Marcus Antoninus rests less on his intellectual attainments than on his employment of them in the service of the state. Gibbon's praise of the Senator Boethius is founded less on his appreciation of the *Consolation of Philosophy*, which he describes as 'a golden volume, not unworthy of the leisure of Plato or Tully', than on the senator's participation in public life. It is his patriotism which wins Gibbon's highest approval: 'A philosopher, liberal of his wealth and parsimonious of his time, might be insensible to the common allurements of ambition, the thirst of gold and employment. And some credit may be due to the asseveration of Boethius, that he had reluctantly obeyed the divine Plato, who enjoins every virtuous citizen to rescue the state from the usurpation of vice and ignorance.'[39] In a like manner, Charlemagne is both praised and blamed for his service to his people and to posterity: 'The inveterate evils of the times were suspended or mollified by his government; but in his institutions I can seldom discover the general views and the immortal spirit of a legislator, who survives himself for the benefit of posterity.'[40] In Gibbon the judgement commonly rests on the contribution the individual has made to the well-being and happiness of his city, nation, empire, and world. He rarely fails to notice in the course of his busy narrative those who by the invention of some art have contributed to the welfare of civilization, and he deplores the fact that human energies are often more forcibly exerted for the destruction of man than for his improvement. In mentioning the importation of silk-worms from China to Byzantium, for example, he remarks that he is not insensible to the benefits of luxury, but considers that if the art of printing, then known in China, had been introduced instead of silk-worms, many invaluable volumes would have been preserved for modern times. Or he will contrast the rapid diffusion of the art of making gunpowder with the slow and painful steps by which reason, tolerance, and virtue spread through the world. Gibbon can hardly be called a Christian, and as an enemy of zeal and superstition in every form he criticizes sharply many of the institutions of Christianity. Yet, characteristically,

[39] iv. 199–200.

[40] v. 285.

the one matter on which he pauses to praise the Church is its civilizing power; and the major fault he finds with it is that its emphasis on happiness in a future life contributed to the real miseries of mankind in this life. He summarizes his criticisms in general observations on the causes of the fall of the empire in the west. Christianity had some influence in the fall of the Roman empire, he writes. 'The clergy successfully preached the doctrine of patience and pusillanimity; the active virtues of society were discouraged; and the last remains of military spirit were buried in the cloister; a large portion of public and private wealth was consecrated to the specious demands of charity and devotion; and the soldiers' pay was lavished on the useless multitudes of both sexes, who could only plead the merits of abstinence and charity.'[41] He also points out that history has shown that whatever might be the claims of Christianity, 'The rage of war, inherent to the human species, could not be healed by the evangelic precepts of charity and peace; and the ambition of Catholic princes has renewed in every age the calamities of hostile contention.'[42] But within the context of his own values and ideals, Gibbon is impartial, and he follows each of these remarks, which have been drawn from widely separated sections of *The Decline and Fall*, with a modification. In the first instance, he writes, 'the pure and genuine influence of Christianity may be traced in its beneficial, though imperfect, effects on the Barbarian proselytes of the North. If the decline of the Roman empire was hastened by the conversion of Constantine, his victorious religion broke the violence of the fall, and mollified the ferocious temper of the conquerors.'[43] And in the second, Christianity is credited with having brought the barbarians within the pale of civil and ecclesiastical Europe.

Gibbon's conviction that mankind may achieve its own happiness and fulfilment by civilizing the globe deserves to be related to Virgil's faith in the civilizing destiny of Rome. Precisely what was so awful about the fall of the Roman empire was that Rome failed to fulfil her great destiny. It is interesting to note that in answering the question of why this happened, Gibbon sees nothing inherently wrong with classical liberalism: had the republicans of Rome achieved the virtue, maintained the patriotism, and striven to attain the wisdom of the best of their species, they would never

[41] iv. 162–3. [42] vi. 165. [43] iv. 163.

have abdicated their freedom and its attendant responsibilities. The remark that the decline of Rome was 'the natural and inevitable effect of immoderate greatness' simply underlines Gibbon's interest in the strenuous, competitive liberty of a republic, which he contrasts with the dull uniformity of the empire. Even if its excessive magnitude had naturally led to its division, under the influence of liberty its virtue would have been preserved in its constituent parts. In turning to his own day Gibbon still maintains the ideals of classical liberalism, and after the vicissitudes of eighteen centuries he finds them once more dominant in the modern republic of Europe:

> . . . a philosopher may be permitted to enlarge his views, and to consider Europe as one great republic, whose various inhabitants have attained almost the same level of politeness and cultivation. The balance of power will continue to fluctuate, and the prosperity of our own or the neighbouring kingdoms may be alternately exalted or depressed; but these partial events cannot essentially injure our general state of happiness, the system of arts, and laws, and manners, which so advantageously distinguish above the rest of mankind, the Europeans and their colonies.[44]

But his study is the fall of Rome where 'the mild and generous influence of liberty' was not preserved. Rome's immoderate greatness, her wealth, luxury, and power, prepared the ground for the tyrants by encouraging uniformity, blunting the edge of responsibility and duty, undermining civic virtue and discouraging the practice of private virtue. The civilizing mission of the republic was usurped first by the tyrants, who perverted it to their own ends, and, secondly, in Gibbon's opinion, by the institution of Christianity. The tyrants, after many centuries, brought about their own destruction; corrupted by their own power, they sought simply the gratification of their own ambitions and passions, instead of the happiness and well-being of mankind. The logical dead-end of tyranny is seen in the horrible parade of Byzantine emperors in Chapter XLVIII. The Christian Church usurped the civilizing mission of free men by substituting revelation for reason. This victory was achieved by the Church in two steps: first, by dividing the spiritual from the temporal, and arrogating to itself

[44] iv. 163.

complete control over the spiritual life of man. As its power grew, the next logical step was the extension of its dominion to temporal affairs as well.

Gibbon sees that it is in the nature of tyranny to corrupt and destroy itself, for the tyrant, he says, by a law of eternal justice is degraded by the vices of his subjects. The emperors had been corrupted by their own power, and they were further punished by the victorious barbarians who exploited and developed every weakness of the state. In a similar fashion, the tyranny of the Church resulted in corruption, and it was further punished by the victorious reformation. Gibbon subscribes to the view that human nature will eventually throw off the shackles of tyranny, and he seeks to support his thesis by pointing to the virtues of the 'republic of Europe' and to the 'indifferent religion' of an enlightened age. There is no such thing as equality of merit or of ability, but man, created capable of freedom and reason, must seek his fulfilment in both. Failure to do so results in slavery to his passions and appetites, political servitude, and the tyranny of superstition. There appears to be operative at the heart of *The Decline and Fall* something very close to the Greek idea of nemesis, and the fourteen agonizing centuries can be regarded as an illustration of what happens when man fails to accept the responsibilities of his nature. The terrifying cost which men must pay for abdicating their freedom and their dignity is measured in centuries of blood and tears. The Ciceronian concept of right reason, combined with the Virgilian faith in Rome's civilizing destiny, provides the base for the dynamics of Gibbon's *The Decline and Fall.*

I should like to suggest now that *The Decline and Fall* can be regarded as an eighteenth-century, secular, prose equivalent of *Paradise Lost.* Its subject is the fall of man from a state of intellectual, spiritual, and political freedom into the darkness of barbarism and servitude of every sort, until, at the end of fourteen centuries, with the Renaissance and the beginning of the Reformation, man begins to emerge into the enlightenment, which, Gibbon felt, characterized his own age.[45] A more careful examination of the main lines of organization and dominant features of the whole

[45] Cf. Lewis P. Curtis, 'Gibbon's Paradise Lost', *The Age of Johnson* (New Haven, 1949), pp. 73–90. This is a seminal article, but the bases for my conclusions differ considerably from those of Mr. Curtis.

will illustrate how closely Gibbon followed this thesis. It is important to remember that in shaping his narrative and evaluating his materials, the historian can do only what they permit. But, as we have seen, in Gibbon's search for a great historical topic he looked for a major theme. In the enormous scope of the decline and fall of Rome he found it: the potential dignity of man, and on this base, the assertion of his right to intellectual and political freedom.

Pursuing the thought that *The Decline and Fall* is a story of fall and redemption, we find that the long history quite naturally and intentionally is divided into two great periods. The first takes us from the age of the Antonines to the death of Heraclius (A.D. 641), the last of the Byzantine emperors who retrieved in any way the name of Rome. This long period, which Gibbon covers in forty-seven chapters, is concerned with the fall of the empire in the west and the progressive slavery and decay of the 'Romans' in the east. At this point we reach a kind of dead centre, and Gibbon pauses to outline his plans for the last two volumes and to explain why he has chosen to continue his history: 'I should have abandoned, without regret, the Greek slaves and their servile historians, had I not reflected that the fate of the Byzantine monarchy is *passively* connected with the most splendid and important revolutions which have changed the state of the world. The space of the lost provinces was immediately replenished with new colonies and rising kingdoms; the active virtues of peace and war deserted from the vanquished to the victorious nations; . . .'[46] Here he begins the transition from his study of the fall of Rome to a concern with the slow and painful steps by which the virtues of civilization and freedom again emerged, this time in modern Europe. For the Greek 'slaves' Gibbon has nothing but contempt. Their external splendour had been altogether lost. 'From the time of Heraclius, the Byzantine theatre is contracted and darkened; the line of empire, which had been defined by the laws of Justinian and the arms of Belisarius, recedes on all sides from our view; the Roman name, the proper subject of our inquiries, is reduced to a narrow corner of Europe, to the lonely suburbs of Constantinople; and the fate of the Greek empire has been compared to that of the Rhine, which loses itself in the sands before its waters can mingle with the ocean.'[47] And the loss of external splendour, he continues,

[46] v. 171. [47] v. 169.

is not compensated by the more prized gifts of virtue and genius: 'the subjects of the Byzantine empire, who assume and dishonour the names both of Greeks and Romans, present a dead uniformity of abject vices, which are neither softened by the weakness of humanity, nor animated by the vigour of memorable crimes'.[48] The extent of the fall is illustrated for the reader by a comparison drawn from Homer. If anyone has missed the thesis which Gibbon has been implicitly developing throughout his long narrative, this comparison makes clear that we have at last reached the very nadir of civilization. 'The freemen of antiquity might repeat, with generous enthusiasm, the sentence of Homer, "that, on the first day of his servitude, the captive is deprived of one half of his manly virtue". But the poet had only seen the effects of civil or domestic slavery, nor could he foretell that the second moiety of manhood must be annihilated by the spiritual despotism which shackles not only the actions but even the thoughts of the prostrate votary. By this double yoke, the Greeks were oppressed by the successors of Heraclius; . . .'[49] A further comparison, between the citizens of Athens in her most flourishing era and those of Constantinople under the successors of Heraclius, is drawn, and the virtues of free men set off in bold relief the ignominy of slaves.

It is characteristic of Gibbon that when he contemplates continuing his history from the death of Heraclius to the final capture of Constantinople by the Turks in 1453, a narrative which takes up the emergence of modern European civilization, he is concerned, as any artist would be, with 'the unity of design' of the whole work. He is aware that he can continue to focus on Constantinople until the last slave of Byzantine tyranny is destroyed or captured, and at the same time illustrate his thesis of the rebirth of human dignity and freedom. He writes: 'Nor will this scope of narrative, the riches and variety of these materials, be incompatible with the unity of design and composition. As, in his daily prayers, the Musulman of Fez or Delhi still turns his face toward the temple of Mecca, the historian's eye shall be always fixed on the city of Constantinople. The excursive line may embrace the wilds of Arabia and Tartary, but the circle will be ultimately reduced to the decreasing limit of the Roman monarchy.'[50] The central comparison here is of special interest. Mecca is, of course,

[48] v. 170. [49] Ibid. [50] v. 171.

the spiritual home of the Mohammedan; and in Gibbon's view, Rome is the spiritual father of European culture. Not the Rome of the popes, but the Rome of the republic and early empire. He no doubt had this in mind when he wrote the last sentence of his narrative, just before the peroration which ends the work: 'and the footsteps of heroes, the relics, not of superstition, but of empire, are devoutly visited by a new race of pilgrims from the remote, and once savage, countries of the North'.[51] Constantinople will continue to be the focus, not because of any intrinsic merit, but only because it preserves the name of Rome until the time when the nations who grew out of the ruins of her greatness had appropriated to themselves, as an essential part of their tradition and culture, the last vestiges of her ancient glory. On this point it is interesting to see a change which Gibbon had planned for a revised edition of his text. He got no farther than page 32 of the first volume, but one notation is important. He planned to change the words, 'to deduce the most important circumstances of its decline and fall: a revolution which will ever be remembered, and is still felt by the nations of the earth',[52] to the more correct and concrete assertion: 'To prosecute the decline and fall of the empire of Rome: of whose language, religion and laws the impression will be long preserved in our own and the neighbouring countries of Europe.'[53] Just as the Roman conquerors of Greece were in turn conquered by the arts and civilization of that extraordinary nation, so the destroyers of Rome, among whom Gibbon numbers the Christians, were won by the spirit of the empire they destroyed. The unity of the whole work still rests on the story of the decline and fall of Rome, but the Roman virtues having deserted to the victorious nations, it is their histories which animate the renaissance of civilization; and Byzantium is henceforth a largely passive spectator of her own destruction.

I have already described the major reason for the fall of Rome and suggested that the first part of *The Decline and Fall* illustrates how Rome was precipitated by just degrees from the abuse to the loss of her freedom. Further support for this thesis is found in Gibbon's note on the first page of the second edition, which he started to revise. 'Should I not have deduced the decline of the

[51] vii. 324–5. [52] i. 1.
[53] Quoted by J. B. Bury, ed., *The Decline and Fall*, i. xxxv.

Empire from the Civil Wars that ensued after the Fall of Nero, or even from the tyranny which succeeded the reign of Augustus? Alas! I should: but of what avail is this tardy knowledge? Where error is irreparable, repentance is useless.'[54] Such a revision would merely have emphasized the implication of these first chapters and underlined the role of Augustus, whose arts and policy subverted the freedom of the Romans. On the other hand, the age of the Antonines has the superior merit of balancing apparent, and in many ways real, prosperity with the unmistakable symptoms of decay.

The main lines of the argument of the first part of *The Decline and Fall* will be treated more fully when we come to discuss Gibbon's narrative technique, and it will be sufficient simply to note here that almost immediately after the death of Marcus Antoninus and the accession of Commodus, the long and melancholy tale of corruption and decay gets under way. The narrative is conducted on three major lines of development, which sometimes meet and mingle, and sometimes are handled separately. The first is focused on the government of the empire and includes the internal political struggles; the characters, actions, and laws of the emperors; and the affairs of the army, an important element since military despotism played a large role in the fall of Rome. The second concerns the growth and corruption of the Christian Church, which not only brought about the abolition of paganism, but also contributed to the civil conflicts of the age and was responsible for the final separation of the East and West, subsequent to the reign of Justinian. The third main line of development concerns the inroads of the barbarians, who in their great migrations simply capitalized on the weakness of the empire. Under the first of these topics, Gibbon illustrates the abuse and loss of political freedom; under the second, the progressive loss of intellectual and spiritual freedom; under the third, the tyranny or anarchy, the licentiousness and chaos, which punish as by a natural law man's failure to accept the challenge of his liberty.

As Gibbon approaches the final enslavement of what is left of the empire, he pauses to consider the history of Roman jurisprudence. The great age of Roman law stretched from the birth of Cicero to the reign of Alexander Severus, but in the last stages of

[54] Ibid.

decline the influence of these noble precepts was feeble indeed. 'The will of a single man, of a child perhaps, was allowed to prevail over the wisdom of ages and the inclinations of millions; and the degenerate Greeks were proud to declare that in his hands alone the arbitrary exercise of legislation could be safely deposited.'[55] This was a time when 'the oracles of jurisprudence were almost mute. The measure of curiosity had been filled; the throne was occupied by tyrants and Barbarians; the active spirits were diverted by religious disputes; and the professors of Rome, Constantinople, and Berytus were humbly content to repeat the lessons of their more enlightened predecessors.'[56] To complete his picture of the servitude of the Greeks, there remains only a discussion of the theological history of the Doctrine of the Incarnation, which Gibbon takes up in the last chapter (XLVII) of the first part. Out of a religious war which lasted 250 years, the last link in the 'chains of dogma' was formed. Various heresies, almost invisible to the eye of reason, were purged with much bloodshed and passion. The Christians, says Gibbon, were more solicitous to explore the nature than to practice the laws of their founder; and the first part of *The Decline and Fall* ends with the most scandalous abuses of the doctrines of the gospels. The reader, like the King of Brobdingnag, is perfectly astonished with the historical account.

The second part of *The Decline and Fall* has the double objective of pursuing the history of the extinction of Rome and bringing us to the threshold of the modern republic of Europe, which Gibbon has compared in its merit and virtue with the federated states of Greece. Against the background of Byzantine history, we follow the rise and fall of the new political and military powers of the Holy Roman Empire, the Saracens, and the Turks. The impact on Europe of the conquests of Genghis Khan and Tamburlaine is treated along with the effects of the great crusades to Jerusalem. The emergence of the nations of France, Germany, Italy, England, Hungary, and Spain develops the history of these ancient Roman provinces to the beginnings of modern times. In his study of the Church, Gibbon discusses the rise of Mohammedanism, the growth of the temporal power of the popes, and the final triumph and effect of the Reformation. The revival of the arts and of the

[55] iv. 451–2.

[56] iv. 456.

study of letters is amply covered up to the time of Petrarch in Italy. The gradual civilizing process operative on the barbarian conquerors of Rome in these centuries provides a sustained contrast with the continued decay of Byzantium.

It is unnecessary to outline the long narrative which brings the reader finally back to Rome in the fifteenth century to see in the ruins of that great capital the visible manifestations of what the revolution of fourteen centuries has meant to the civilized world. It will be sufficient to point out how in the opening chapters of the second part of *The Decline and Fall* Gibbon concentrates on the stirring of new growth, on the beginning of rebirth in Europe. Everywhere, except in Constantinople, the process of renaissance is beginning. We are presented first with a single chapter narrative of the lives of the Byzantine emperors up to the year 1204. Six hundred years pass rapidly before our eyes, and, although the memory is severely taxed by this chapter, the thesis Gibbon is developing and his reason for selecting it are clear. The subject is really the effects of tyranny and slavery, and it provides a base of vice and ignominy which will contrast sharply with the growing freedom of the rest of Europe. The reader's sensibilities are almost offended by the long parade of inhuman torture and viciousness. Among the sixty emperors only John Comnenus was beneficent and pure. Only a handful of emperors balanced their vices with their virtues: the rest, Gibbon says, posterity would desire to forget. The patterns of despotism are inexorable, and a fairly strong stomach is needed to endure the tales of castration, blinding, cutting out of tongues, burning victims alive in the furnaces of the baths, cutting off of noses, tales which illustrate the manners by which the tyrants attained or secured their thrones. If the tyrants were degraded by the vices of their subjects, the subjects had contracted all the vices of slaves.

Gibbon then proceeds to discuss the worship of images, a practice which contributed to the antagonism between the West and the East. Although this discussion is concerned with the scandalous abuse of Christianity, the references by which Gibbon illustrates it are more frequently drawn from what became the future state of affairs rather than from past history. In writing the first part of *The Decline and Fall,* wherever possible Gibbon embraced the occasion to breathe the pure and invigorating air of the republic. In composing the second part, he was happy to illustrate the genesis of his own philosophic age by examples drawn from it.

Other signs of the emergence of new life and vitality are found everywhere in these opening chapters. On the same matter of the conflict over the worship of images, Gibbon writes: 'The liberty of Rome, which had been oppressed by the arms and the arts of Augustus, was rescued, after seven hundred and fifty years of servitude, from the persecution of Leo the Isaurian.'[57] But this and other examples are only the first faint stirrings of the revival of the human spirit: 'When the sovereignty of the Greek emperors was extinguished, the ruins of Rome presented the sad image of depopulation and decay; her slavery was an habit, her liberty an accident: the effect of superstition, and the object of her own amazement and terror.'[58] The story of the renaissance is a long and in many ways a painful one, which, in Gibbon's narrative, covers almost eight centuries, but the crucial thing to note is that it has started.

It is hoped that this brief *résumé* will illustrate the meaning which Gibbon found in his materials, and the 'argument' of *The Decline and Fall.* The tremendous pageant of human life exhibited within the pages of this enormous work is guided and conducted, without violating the truth of historical detail, to illustrate in the boldest and most memorable way that the dignity and nobility of the human spirit are possible only under conditions of political and spiritual freedom. This is the epic theme, and it is 'to the height of this great argument' that Gibbon has aspired.

There remains for this chapter a brief consideration of a common misconception of *The Decline and Fall,* one which results from taking Gibbon's description of the age of the Antonines as a portrait of his ideal state of society. It is not my intention to repeat arguments already advanced to show that, far from being an ideal period, this age is noted by Gibbon for *apparent* well-being and real decay; but comments such as those by Leslie Stephen should be met. In quoting the famous passage, 'If a man were called to fix the period . . . when the human race was most happy and prosperous . . .', Leslie Stephen points out that Gibbon's

[57] v. 262. [58] v. 263.

ideal state of society is 'the death-like trance of an enlightened despotism'.

He does not sympathize with the periods marked by vehement ebullitions of human passion breaking down the frozen crust of society, evolving new forms of religion, art, and philosophy, and in the process, producing struggles, excitement, and disorder, but with the periods of calm stagnation, when nobody believes strongly, feels warmly, or acts energetically. A peaceful acquiescence in the established order, not an heroic struggle towards fuller satisfaction of all human instincts, is his ideal. Equilibrium, at whatever sacrifice obtained, is the one political good; and his millennium can be reached rather by men ceasing to labour than by their obtaining a full fruition.[59]

In replying to these remarks, we might quote Gibbon's lament at the end of the entire work, and hear him use the metaphor of stagnation: 'In Rome the voice of freedom and discord is no longer heard; and, instead of the foaming torrent, a smooth and stagnant lake reflects the image of idleness and servitude.'[60] Or we can listen to his praise of Athens in her greatest period, hardly one of calm stagnation: 'Athens, after her Persian triumphs, adopted the philosophy of Ionia and the rhetoric of Sicily; and these studies became the patrimony of a city whose inhabitants, about thirty thousand males, condensed, within the period of a single life, the genius of ages and millions.'[61] We might recall Gibbon's comments on strenuous competitive liberty wherein emulation is productive of the greatest improvements of mankind, or his remark that in the Reformation freedom and knowledge expanded *all* the faculties of mankind.[62] Equilibrium? Yes, but the balance of power and interest between an aspiring prince, a stubborn Commons, and a martial nobility is rarely productive of calm stagnation. True, Gibbon had no sympathy for such 'vehement ebullitions of human passion breaking down the frozen crust of society' as seen in the French Revolution. Of this violent upheaval he has made a typical comment. In a letter to his stepmother he says: 'In the moving picture of the World, you cannot be indifferent to the strange Revolution which has humbled all that was

[59] *English Thought in the Eighteenth Century* (2 vols., London, 1927), i. 447–8.
[60] vii. 298.
[61] iv. 261.
[62] v. 253.

high and exalted all that was low in France. The irregular and lively spirit of the Nation has disgraced their liberty, and instead of building a free constitution they have only exchanged Despotism for Anarchy. . . . Burke, if I remember right, is no favorite of yours; but there is surely much eloquence and much sense in his book.'[63] But his horror of the revolution in France should not be read to mean that he accepted as his ideal state of society the 'death-like trance of an enlightened despotism'. The purpose of organized society was, in Gibbon's view, to provide the blessings of peace and justice, which neither anarchy nor despotism can supply.

Leslie Stephen has missed in *The Decline and Fall* the spirit which turns what otherwise could be considered 'an anatomical demonstration of the dead framework of society' into a dynamic study of the destiny of man, viewed as Cicero and Tacitus might see it if they were capable of sharing the Olympian heights which 2,000 years of history opened to Gibbon. His thesis that man can develop his own powers and his civilization under the conditions of freedom provides the energy which activates his portraits and shows the philosophic historian's conception of an underlying law of history.

[63] *The Letters of Edward Gibbon*, iii. 227.

III · THE STRUCTURE

In turning from the argument of *The Decline and Fall* to a study of Gibbon's art, one finds that the structure of his great work is among its most impressive features. The history was composed over a period of roughly twenty years. There is ample evidence to demonstrate that the topic and scope of the undertaking were continually growing in his mind; yet our study of the great theme of the history has shown that there is throughout the entire work a remarkable homogeneity of thought. In considering the structure, we shall find that although the first volumes were published many years before the last were even written, there is a unity of form in the whole which is nothing less than astonishing.

His own comments on his planning of the work are few, but we have an interesting letter he wrote to Lord Sheffield, who had misgivings about his publication of the first volume before the others were completed. Gibbon replies: 'Your apprehensions of a precipitate work &c., are perfectly groundless. I should be much more addicted to a contrary extreme. The *head* is now printing? true: but it was wrote last year and the year before; the first Chapter has been composed *de nouveau three times*; the second *twice*, and all the others have undergone reviews, corrections, &c. As to the tail, it is perfectly formed. . . .'[1] It is quite probable that 'the tail' as we now have it differs from the conception he then had in his mind. In the preface to the first volume he adumbrated a design for the entire history, even though he did not then presume to promise its execution. He divides the 'memorable series of revolutions' into three major periods which deal with (1) the fall of the empire in the West; (2) the reign of Justinian and revival in the West under Charlemagne; and (3) the six and a half centuries from the revival of the West to the capture of Constantinople by the Turks in 1453. This outline was not abandoned, but it was transcended as Gibbon, working on the later

[1] *The Letters of Edward Gibbon*, J. E. Norton, ed. (3 vols., New York, 1956), ii. 81.

section of his history, gained greater perspective and a deeper understanding of the meaning of the whole. Indeed, one can assert that the structure of the work remained fluid and unset until the final paragraph was written. The outline which accompanied his first volume was designed to supply a context, to give the reader a broad grasp of the salient features of the larger work. The experience of composition, however, opened new vistas: 'A long while ago, when I contemplated the distant prospect of my work, I gave you and myself some hopes of landing in England last Autumn; but alas! when autumn drew near, hills began to rise on hills, Alps on Alps. . . .'[2] And as he progressed in the execution he saw that the overall structure should be divided into two major periods instead of three, the first dealing with the fall, and the second with the recovery, of man. This design he was able to superimpose on what had already been published by the manner in which he composed the last part of the history. A closer look at the structure of the completed work will substantiate my point.

The whole history of the decline and fall of Rome is told in seventy-one carefully wrought chapters. The first three, which present a survey of the Roman world in the age of the Antonines, are static and largely descriptive of the culture of the Romans in this great age. The last three chapters follow immediately upon the capture of Constantinople by the Turks in 1453, and we return to Rome, where Gibbon traces the history of that city from the twelfth to the fifteenth century. He concludes his history with a survey of the ruins of Rome. These three-chapter units at the beginning and the end provide a frame for the action which Gibbon relates in the body of the work. Within this unified context the history is divided into two major parts. The first part, which considers the decline of the Romans into slavery (Chapters IV–XLVII), reaches its climax in Chapter XXXVI, with the accession of Odoacer, the first barbarian king of Italy. The second part, which brings us to the Renaissance and the capture of Constantinople (Chapters XLVIII–LXVIII), reaches its climax in Chapter LX, where the forces of the growing 'republic of Europe' are brought into direct contact with the 'slaves' of the expiring

[2] *The Letters of Edward Gibbon*, J. E. Norton, ed. (3 vols., New York, 1956), iii. 59.

empire of Rome. This chapter describes the conquest and sack of Constantinople by the crusaders in the year 1204. The climax of each part is followed, after a brief amplification, by a digression. In the digression of Part I, Gibbon examines the causes for the fall of the empire in the West and questions whether they are still operative in modern Europe. In the digression of Part II, which follows his discussion of the consequences of the crusades, he takes up the origin and history of a leading family in the cultural revival of Europe, the family of Courtenay. The pivotal centre of the work, at the beginning of Chapter XLVIII, where he describes his plans for the last two volumes, has already been considered in my second chapter. Let us turn to a closer examination of the climax of each part.

The last Roman emperor in the West was a man whose name, by a curious coincidence, combined the appellations of Rome's great founders: Romulus and Augustus. Of Augustulus, Gibbon writes: 'a youth recommended only by his beauty, would be the least entitled to the notice of posterity, if his reign, which was marked by the extinction of the Roman empire in the West, did not leave a memorable aera in the history of mankind'.[3] He is supplanted by the barbarian king Odoacer, who reigned, Gibbon says, 'over a people who had once asserted their just superiority above the rest of mankind'.[4] At this point he quietly recalls the age of Roman virtue when 'the provinces were subject to the arms, and the citizens to the laws, of the republic'; and the final fall of the West is made darker by memory of past greatness. The decay of the Roman spirit is his theme at this, the climax of the first part of the history. Two chapters, however, intervene between the climax and Gibbon's digression titled, 'General Observations on the Fall of the Roman Empire in the West'. They have the function of amplifying and completing the picture, and bringing it into focus before he undertakes an analysis of what has been related thus far. The first of these chapters describes the rise of monasticism, the conversion of the barbarians to Christianity and Arianism, and their eventual conversion to orthodoxy; in the other, he considers the fate of three important Roman provinces in the West which he had not already covered: Gaul, Spain, and

[3] *The History of the Decline and Fall of the Roman Empire*, J. B. Bury, ed. (7 vols., London, 1896–1900), iv. 51.

[4] iv. 53.

Britain. The climax in Chapter XXXVI had concluded with a long paragraph on the miserable state of Italy. The two-chapter amplification shows us the triumph of the new religion and the emergence of the French monarchy under Clovis. The digression, in its general observations, looks both backward, to assess the history which had preceded the fall of the West, and forward, to apply the lessons of Rome's fall to modern Europe. The succeeding chapters in Part I of the history extend through the reign of Justinian and the temporary restoration of the empire by the conquests of Belisarius, to the anticlimax, the completion of the slavery of the eastern empire. Significantly enough, Gibbon ends Part I with a study of the theological doctrine of the incarnation and the separation of the oriental sects from the pale of the Catholic Church. Out of the turmoil of appalling religious conflict came the uniformity of orthodoxy: 'Before the end of the seventh century, the creed of the incarnation, which had been defined at Rome and Constantinople, was uniformly preached in the remote islands of Britain and Ireland; the same ideas were entertained, or rather the same words were repeated, by all the Christians whose liturgy was performed in the Greek or the Latin tongue.'[5] Gibbon then disengages the oriental sects from the union of the Latin and Greek churches, and Part I ends with the near death of the spirit of Rome.

Part II has the double burden of illustrating the emergence of modern Europe and the final extinction of the Roman empire. Here we find in the structure a striking parallel to the first part. Gibbon's 'excursive line' embraces much: the rise and fall of Mohammedanism, the incursions of the Normans, the conquests of Charlemagne. But in the crusaders' sack of Constantinople the two main themes cross each other. One more step down is recorded in the history of the loss of Roman power; and the emerging civilization of Europe, which meets and mingles with the vestiges of the old in the most formidable way, is seen clearly in the ascendant. The account of the siege closes with a description of some of the priceless statues destroyed by the conquerors, and with Gibbon's sober, humanistic reflection on a great cultural loss: 'Of the writings of antiquity many that still existed in the twelfth century are now lost. But the pilgrims were not solicitous to save or transport the volumes of an unknown tongue; . . . the literature

[5] v. 143.

of the Greeks had almost centred in the metropolis; and, without computing the extent of our loss, we may drop a tear over the libraries that have perished in the triple fire of Constantinople.'[6] The concluding paragraph of the climactic chapter in Part I had described the miserable state of Italy. Here, the loss to modern civilization is Gibbon's concern. He balances the crusaders' destruction of works of art, however, with a remark that the Greeks, who have recorded their losses, overlooked the progress of the Latins. And the clearest indication of this progress, and of the fact that he was deliberately interested in emphasizing it, is found in the passage with which he introduces the pillage of Constantinople: 'Their cruelty and lust were moderated by the authority of the chiefs and feelings of the soldiers; for we are no longer describing an irruption of northern savages; and, however ferocious they might still appear, time, policy, and religion had civilized the manners of the French and still more of the Italians.'[7] We might recall Gibbon's remark at the beginning of the second part, that 'the active virtues of peace and war' passed over to the new nations. The climax of Part II is a dramatic representation of this thesis.

Just as in Part I, Gibbon follows his climax by a short amplification. In this case he describes the period of the empire of the Latins in Constantinople, the recovery of the city by the Greeks, and the consequences of the crusades. With the picture completed he gives the reader a brief digression on the family of Courtenay. The appropriateness of the digression in the first part is obvious, and on reflection it is apparent that a digression on an important family in the now emerging 'republic of Europe' is admirably suited to the theme of the second part.

Constantinople was recovered by the Greeks in 1261. Almost 200 years must elapse before the empire and religion of Constantinople are trampled in the dust by the armies of Mohammed the Second. But that the crusades constitute the true climax of the second part of the history can be seen by the meaning which Gibbon finds in them. They were in great part responsible for the revival of culture in Europe:

The estates of the barons were dissipated, and their race was often

[6] vi. 412.   [7] vi. 406.

extinguished, in these costly and perilous expeditions. Their poverty extorted from their pride those charters of freedom which unlocked the fetters of the slave, secured the farm of the peasant and the shop of the artificer, and gradually restored a substance and a soul to the most numerous and useful part of the community. The conflagration which destroyed the tall and barren trees of the forest gave air and scope to the vegetation of the smaller and nutritive plants of the soil.[8]

And in the sack of Constantinople they irretrievably weakened an already degenerate people. Two centuries later, in the death throes of Byzantium, some of the ancient virtue and heroism which centuries before had paved the way for Roman greatness are seen again, but only among a handful of citizens. The rest were unwilling even to defend their city. The *coup de grâce* is administered in 1453, and the empire of Rome is no more.

Properly speaking, Gibbon's history is completed at this point. He has accomplished all that he has promised to do. But he places three chapters between the fall of Constantinople and the conclusion of his work. These chapters serve the valuable function of bringing the entire history into a strongly unified, clear perspective. The transitional passage which leads into this amplification is worth quoting.

> The name of Rome must yet command our involuntary respect; the climate (whatsoever may be its influence) was no longer the same; the purity of blood had been contaminated through a thousand channels; but the venerable aspect of her ruins, and the memory of past greatness, rekindled a spark of the national character. The darkness of the middle ages exhibits some scenes not unworthy of our notice. Nor shall I dismiss the present work till I have reviewed the state and revolutions of the ROMAN CITY, which acquiesced under the absolute dominion of the Popes about the same time Constantinople was enslaved by the Turkish arms.[9]

The first two chapters of this final section are narratives dealing with the development of the temporal powers of the popes, their retirement to Avignon, and return to Rome. Also taken up are the institutions and the various rulers of the city, along with the extraordinary tale of the abortive efforts by the Tribune Rienzi to restore the freedom and government of Rome. With the failure of Rienzi, and the return of the popes, the last spark of Roman free-

[8] vi. 446.

[9] vii. 209–10.

dom died. Neither Rienzi nor Petrarch was able to reanimate the degenerate Romans of his day with the vigour, the virtue, or the magnanimity which characterized the Romans of old. As the last sputterings of the ancient fire are extinguished, a comparison with former greatness is suggested, and the final chapter of the work takes us to a consideration of the ruins of Rome as seen in the fifteenth century. The concluding chapter is directly connected by the most awesome comparison with the opening chapter on the magnitude of the empire. The extent of the fall, which taxes the human imagination and memory to the utmost, is made concrete and even tangible, by the vivid description of Poggius:

> The path of victory is obliterated by vines, and the benches of the senators are concealed by a dunghill. Cast your eyes on the Palatine hill, and seek, among the shapeless and enormous fragments, the marble theatre, the obelisks, the colossal statues, the porticoes of Nero's palace: survey the other hills of the city, the vacant space is interrupted only by ruins and gardens. The forum of the Roman people, where they assembled to enact their laws and elect their magistrates, is now inclosed for the cultivation of pot-herbs or thrown open for the reception of swine and buffaloes. The public and private edifices, that were founded for eternity, lie prostrate, naked, and broken, like the limbs of a mighty giant; and the ruin is the more visible, from the stupendous relics that have survived the injuries of time and fortune.[10]

From this appalling contrast Gibbon turns to a consideration of the causes for the destruction of these monuments. The history has been concerned with the lives, the actions, and the deaths of men and their governments, he remarks, and at the end we shall consider the destruction of even the most durable of their creations. His careful discussion of four principal causes for the ruin of the monuments of Rome has the effect of controlling and disciplining the strong emotion one feels on viewing them with the understanding which fourteen centuries of history have given. The exquisite lament on the vicissitudes of fortune by Poggius is followed by Gibbon's consideration of the brevity of human existence. 'The art of man is able to construct monuments far more permanent than the narrow span of his own existence; yet these monuments, like himself, are perishable and frail; and, in the

[10] vii. 302.

boundless annals of time, his life and his labours must equally be measured as a fleeting moment.'[11]

The functions of the last three chapters are to make the transition from the narrative of the action to the picture of the whole, and to do it in a way which will amplify and bring into full perspective this picture. The reader's emotions are involved so that he is fully receptive to the meaning of the pageant, yet his passions are controlled so that they do not interfere with an intellectual apprehension of the conclusion. The entire spectacle of *The Decline and Fall* suddenly appears before his mind, and it can be viewed now *sub specie aeternitatis*. The dynamic and vital energies of Gibbon's narrative are caught and held in suspension, and all the parts of the work are seen in harmonious and balanced relation to each other. Fourteen centuries appear as a single moment; yet it is a moment vibrant with life. The Roman empire is dead and buried, but its spirit still lives in the monuments which have survived the ravages of time, and it lives in the new race of pilgrims from remote and once savage countries of the North, through whose eyes we take a final look at the ruins. Above all, it continues to live in the long Roman history which has just been completed.

There is one last step before Gibbon gives the final form to his great achievement. The artist must disengage himself from the subject: 'It was among the ruins of the Capitol that I first conceived the idea of a work which has amused and exercised near twenty years of my life, and which, however inadequate to my own wishes, I finally deliver to the curiosity and candour of the public.'[12] The orator has stepped down from the podium. His listeners silently depart.

Readers have generally noted an oratorical quality in Gibbon's prose, and we have his own testimony that he carefully tried out his paragraphs by ear before he put them down on paper. What has already been said about the structure of the work might lead the reader to suspect that in composing his history Gibbon had in mind the rhetoric of a classical oration. Cicero thought of historical composition in terms of oratory, and Gibbon himself has given us a lead in the matter by associating the writing of history with the art of speaking.

[11] vii. 305.

[12] vii. 325.

In the republics of Greece and Rome, the art of speaking was the powerful engine of patriotism or ambition; and the schools of rhetoric poured forth a colony of statesmen and legislators. When the liberty of a public debate was suppressed, the orator, in the honourable profession of an advocate, might plead the cause of innocence and justice; he might abuse his talents in the more profitable trade of panegyric; and the same precepts continued to dictate the fanciful declamations of the sophist and the chaster beauties of historical composition.[13]

Cicero notes, however, that there seem to be no independent directions from the rhetoricians for the writing of history, and makes a few obvious remarks on how histories generally have been handled. It is when we turn to Aristotle that we find a suggestion of the form which approximates that of Gibbon's *Decline and Fall.* In Aristotle's threefold division of rhetoric there is, first, the deliberative address to a popular assembly, discussing the expediency of a proposal for the future; second, the forensic address to a court, discussing the justice of a deed in the past; and third, the panegyric or *epideictic* address, commemorating the significance of a present occasion. *The Decline and Fall* clearly belongs in the last category. The word *panegyric* is an inadequate equivalent for the Greek word *epideictic,* although it is satisfactory so far as it goes. It does suggest the nature of the abuse to which Gibbon referred in his remarks, for the panegyric could easily fall into extravagant or servile praise. But we can get closer to the Aristotelian term if we think of Pericles' funeral oration for the Athenian dead of the Peloponnesian war. We note also that Aristotle says: 'The epideictic style is especially suited to written compositions.'[14] In the study of history Gibbon drew from the tradition of the 'philosophe'; in the selection of theme and determination of the size and scope of *The Decline and Fall* he was animated by the spirit of the epic; and he gave his work the form of an epideictic oration. It is a commemorative address on the fate of the Roman empire. The care which Gibbon lavished on the structure of the larger units supports this thesis, and a brief examination of the proposition, exordium, narration, and peroration will further clarify the form of the history.

[13] iv. 262.

[14] John Henry Freese (trans.), *The 'Art' of Rhetoric* (Loeb Classical Library [Cambridge, 1939]), III. xii. 6.

The proposition of the entire undertaking is stated in the first paragraph: the decline and fall of the Roman empire is 'a revolution which will ever be remembered, and is still felt by the nations of the earth'. Not proof but illustration is the burden of the epideictic speech, and such a proposition is consequently appropriate. As for the *exordium,* Aristotle says: 'In epideictic speeches, the sources of the exordia are praise and blame', and as the beginning of the speech, the exordium should pave the way for what follows. The survey of the age of the Antonines in its careful distribution of praise and blame is the perfect exordium of the epideictic oration. The keynote of the whole is struck: the balance between prosperity and tyranny. The theme is implied; it is to be the effects of the loss of freedom.

> The fatal moment was perhaps approaching, when some licentious youth, or jealous tyrant, would abuse, to the destruction, that absolute power which they [the Antonines] had exerted for the benefit of their people. The ideal restraints of the senate and the laws might serve to display the virtues, but could never correct the vices, of the emperor. The military force was a blind and irresistible instrument of oppression; and the corruption of Roman manners would always supply flatterers eager to applaud, and ministers prepared to serve, the fear or the avarice, the lust or the cruelty, of their masters.[15]

The orator can praise this period as one in which the human race was most happy and prosperous, and he can also make the ominous and terrible remark that: 'The slave of Imperial despotism, whether he was condemned to drag his gilded chain in Rome and the senate, or to wear out a life of exile on the barren rock of Seriphus, or the frozen banks of the Danube, expected his fate in silent despair.'[16]

The various partitions and confirmations of the great body of the history are too numerous for description. Some of them have already been touched upon in my analysis of the structure. I should remind the reader, however, that in true classical fashion Gibbon approaches his peroration by means of an amplification which considers the history of the city of Rome until it, too, acquiesced under absolute dominion about the same time as Constantinople. In the classical peroration, the orator assists his audience's final assimilation of his subject by recapitulating his

[15] *The Decline and Fall,* i. 78–79. [16] i. 82.

major points, and then he disengages himself from it. The final paragraph of *The Decline and Fall* is just such a peroration.

Gibbon himself is the orator, and, in this role, he does not try to exclude himself from the oration. On the contrary, he outlines his plans, tells us the difficulties he has encountered, describes the methods he is using, and explains the inadequacies of his materials. Far from aspiring to the art which conceals art, Gibbon uses his oratorical position as a centring and focusing device; it is an important structural element of the whole. It gives the work a sense of unity and completeness which sustains the reader until the oration is actually finished and its completed form can be apprehended. The orator and his point of view control and discipline the enormous variety of the work until all the parts are in place.

It has been said that Gibbon views the gigantic spectacle of the fall of Rome exclusively from the Roman forum, and it is true that the final glimpse of the subject as a whole is centred in the ruins of the capital. But Gibbon's mind during the course of the narrative hovers over a map of the Mediterranean, descending now to Rome, now to Carthage or to Constantinople to relate particular events and describe particular scenes. He was separated in time by eighteen to three centuries from the periods he was describing, and most of the countries in which the actions took place he knew only from accounts in various books. He had been to Rome, of course, and the deep impression of that city never left him, but the deserts of Arabia and the Caucasian mountains, not to mention the wilds of Tartary and the frozen banks of the Vistula, were utterly foreign to his personal experience. It is through the eyes of travellers and adventurers, whose impressions he carefully checks against each other, that his mind's eye delineates the major features of most of the places where the actions of *The Decline and Fall* are laid. Wherever possible the accounts of classical writers and of those contemporary with the events being considered are used, but a certain detachment is the natural result of Gibbon's distance from his materials. The intervening 'atmosphere' of time and space often filters out all but the most distinguishing features. One example from hundreds will suffice: 'The strangers retreated to their ships, but the populous sea-coast poured forth a multitude of boats; the waters of the Po were so deeply infected with blood that during six years the public prejudice abstained from the fish of the river; and the institution of an annual feast perpetuated the worship of images and the abhorrence of the Greek tyrant.'[17] Yet, where his materials afford sufficient data, and when the importance of an action requires our presence on the scene, Gibbon descends from this large view to relate in considerable detail the particulars of a specific action. There are times when he deliberately confines the reader's attention to heighten the suspense and excitement of an action. In the siege of Rome by the Goths, we man the ramparts with the soldiers of Belisarius and look out over the hostile troops which cover the surrounding plain. On the Persian expedition of Julian, our view is confined to the camp and the plans of the imperial army; as the action proceeds, we are as ignorant as the Romans about the meaning of the ominous silence of the plains and about the intentions of the Persian king. The deliberate limitation of point of view vitalizes the narrative and helps bridge the centuries between the audience and the action Gibbon is describing. He permits us to share, almost to experience, the passions of the actors in the spectacle; but he never loses himself or lets his reader get lost in the heat of a particular action, lest he forget the perspective of the whole. This perspective is obtained from the Olympian heights of Gibbon's own enlightened age.

Another element contributes to Gibbon's detachment from his material. The aim of his history is moral and philosophical instruction, and as the various actions contribute to an understanding of the overall theme, their significance in this relation is emphasized. If one considers the great scenes in *The Decline and Fall*, those most memorable for the vigour and clear detail of their action, he will see that each is distinguished by the importance it bears to the main burden of the narrative. The sacking of Constantinople by the crusaders or the Turks, the triumph of Belisarius over the Vandals at Carthage, or the crossing of the Euphrates by the troops of Julian are dramatic representations of the main ideas of Gibbon's thesis, and they provide material both for the formulation of those ideas and for their illustration. Fixed in the reader's memory by their intrinsic drama and passion, they are secure anchors to hold the more abstract commentary in place.

[17] v. 261–2.

The most awful spectacle in the history of mankind required a dignity of tone worthy of the greatness of what Rome had been. Gibbon records in his *Memoirs*: 'Many experiments were made before I could hit the middle tone between a dull chronicle and a rhetorical declamation: three times did I compose the first chapter, and twice the second and third, before I was tolerably satisfied with their effect.'[18] But once establishing a lofty, dignified tone, he directs his prose forward, one long period following another, with all the precision, discipline, and order of a Roman general manœuvring his legions. His role as orator affords him magnificent control. The sentences are generally long and carefully balanced; the diction is solid and weighty, depending to a great extent on words with Latin roots; and the metaphors and similes are drawn from the actions of heroes. Literary overtones arise from the fresh application of familiar phrases from classical and heroic literature; the rhythm of the prose is suited to reception by the ear; and in general, the tone maintains the nobility and grandeur of the theme. The tone is saved from being monotonous by the discrepancy between the dignity of the theme and the nature of the specific actions which make up the narrative of the work. More often than not, *The Decline and Fall* is concerned with 'the crimes and follies of mankind', with the abuse of human dignity and reason, and with the loss of freedom. The subject of its pages is what man has been contrasted with what man might have been. The result is a continued tension between the ideal and the real, between man's potential dignity as it was realized in the great days of the Roman republic and his real depravity as recorded in fourteen centuries of strife and turmoil. Irony is the chief product of this tension which opens up to Gibbon the entire spectrum of satire.

Not only does the orator vary and modulate his tone according to the nature of his material; his role is also seen clearly in the brilliant transitional passages. If the chapters of this work constitute the bricks of the edifice, surely these paragraphs are the mortar. A student of writing can scarcely find superior examples of the art of transition. They skilfully assess the significance of what has just passed and of what is to come. They modulate the

[18] *The Memoirs of the Life of Edward Gibbon*, G. B. Hill, ed. (New York, 1900), p. 190.

tone to the appropriate level of different actions, and they bring into the sharpest possible focus the relation of the parts to each other. In his transitions he comments not only on the subjects he is concerned with, but also on the manner of treatment he has selected, why he has selected it, and the value the reader can expect or should have derived from his account. Everywhere there is a brilliant clarity which can result only from superb intellectual discipline:

> After pursuing, above six hundred years, the fleeting Caesars of Constantinople and Germany, I now descend, in the reign of Heraclius, on the eastern borders of the Greek monarchy. While the state was exhausted by the Persian war, and the Church was distracted by the Nestorian and Monophysite sects, Mahomet, with the sword in one hand and the Koran in the other, erected his throne on the ruins of Christianity and of Rome. The genius of the Arabian prophet, the manners of his nation, and the spirit of his religion involve the causes of the decline and fall of the Eastern empire; and our eyes are curiously intent on one of the most memorable revolutions which have impressed a new and lasting character on the nations of the globe.[19]

Even in the narrative itself we are conscious of the narrator, who often interjects such remarks as the following: 'A repetition of such capricious brutality, without connection or design, would be tedious and disgusting; and I shall content myself with some events of the twelfth century, which represent the state of the popes and the city.'[20] Or he will introduce a brief digression with the words: 'From the paths of blood, and such is the history of nations, I cannot refuse to turn aside to gather some flowers of science or virtue.'[21] These interjections dramatize the relationship between his audience and himself, and they are, consequently, one more source of interest.

Our consciousness of the narrator is further vivified by his use of an important organizational principle. In his *Memoirs* Gibbon wrote: 'It was not till after many designs, and many trials that I preferred, as I still prefer, the method of grouping my picture by nations; and the seeming neglect of chronological order is surely compensated by the superior merits of interest and perspicuity.'[22]

[19] v. 311.
[20] vii. 216.
[21] vi. 227.
[22] p. 224.

Gibbon groups his picture by nations and also by subject. Although such organization is fairly common in historical writing, the manner in which he uses it and the various effects he is able to achieve with it are not common. In discussing the conduct of a memorial oration, Aristotle specifically points out that 'in the epideictic style the narrative should not be consecutive, but disjointed'.[23] A consecutive narrative of all the facts is difficult to remember, and because the art of the epideictic speaker is to illustrate the reality, the quality, and the significance of actions, he should more properly group his facts. 'From some facts a man may be shown to be courageous, from others wise or just.'[24] Chronology is sacrificed, but the understanding is increased. Narrative is necessary, of course, but even in the conduct of narrative Gibbon selects and chooses, dwelling at length on a short period of time, or covering decades in a paragraph. As G. M. Young has suggested, Fielding may have given him the lead in this respect.[25] In the opening of the second book of *Tom Jones,* Fielding writes: 'When any extraordinary scene presents itself . . . we shall spare no pains nor paper to open it at large to our readers; but if whole years should pass without producing anything worthy his notice, we shall not be afraid of a chasm in our history, but shall hasten on to matters of consequence, and leave such periods of time totally unobserved.' Gibbon was addressing his own enlightened age, and the interest and taste of his audience as well as his own criteria of value determine the way he groups his picture and conducts his narrative. A brief example, drawn from the first part of *The Decline and Fall,* will illustrate how, in the management of the larger elements of his history, Gibbon achieves unusual interest and perspicuity by a thoughtful rather than chronological distribution of materials. Even though Gibbon more frequently groups his picture in the second part of the history, I have drawn my example from the first part in order to illustrate also how he leads into a growing and complicated story the various elements which form its significant parts. It is drawn from the opening narrative, which occupies Chapters IV–XXIV.

With the exordium behind him, in which he has presented a picture of the Roman world in the period of its greatest prosperity

[23] *Rhetoric,* III. xvi. [24] Ibid.

[25] *Gibbon* (Edinburgh, 1932), p. 144.

and power, he devotes four chapters to a chronological account of roughly seventy years of decay so rapid that the empire is brought to the edge of utter dissolution. Before continuing his narrative, however, he pauses to consider in two chapters the barbarian nations who were to punish the weakness of Rome. One chapter describes the manners, morals, and military forces of the Germans, and the other is concerned with the Persians. In both, he considers the background of these barbarians and their previous collisions with the forces of Rome, but his subject is the characteristic qualities of the people or nations involved. (Later in the work we will find him making a similar study of the manners of pastoral nations.) Returning to the narrative, we find that the characters of the barbarians have been drawn, and suspense has been built up until in the tenth chapter, Gibbon releases the barbarian hordes on the provinces. This chapter unites all that has gone before, and in the twenty years covered by it, we see the effects of the preceding decline.

Four chapters (XI–XIV) which comprise the next unit of the work are devoted to the restoration of Roman power by the princes of Illyria. They bring the narrative to the rise of Constantine and the beginning of his reign. Gibbon concludes Chapter XIV with a characteristic assessment of what he has related. The rhythm of the orator's progress is set by periods of movement followed by moments of appraisal. Then he considers, in one of his most famous chapters, the origin and progress of the Christian religion in the early days of the empire. He inquires why Christianity spread so rapidly and how extensively it was disseminated, rather than into the various stages of its growth. Characteristically, he has excluded all reference to Christianity prior to this chapter, which introduces the subject precisely at the moment of its greatest relevance to the story of the decline of Rome. It is followed by a study of the conduct of the Roman government towards the Christians from the time of Nero to that of Constantine; but, having introduced this new element into the larger study of the fate of Rome, Gibbon is now content to suspend further narration of the history of the church until he has covered in three chapters (XVII–XIX) the foundation of Constantinople and the reign of Constantine and his immediate successors. A discussion of the impact of Christianity on these events is now possible and valuable, just as an understanding of the governmental affairs of Constantinople now colours the history of the Church. The various lines of development are fully enmeshed in the succeeding chapter (XX), which is concerned with the conversion of Constantine and culminates in the legal establishment of the Christian or Catholic Church. With the affairs of state and the affairs of the Church now inseparably joined, one more chapter is needed to consider the theological controversies which raged over the doctrine of the Trinity and affected alike the citizen, the saint, and the soldier.

At this point Julian the Apostate appears on the scene. Every reader of *The Decline and Fall* has been impressed by the power of this unique figure, and much of it is surely due to the nature of the man and the times in which he lived. Much more, however, results from Gibbon's artistic skill in capitalizing on each detail which history has allowed, to heighten and dramatize the significance of his reign. All major elements of Gibbon's narrative have, by this time, been introduced. The government and the armies of the empire have been studied. The capital has been moved to Constantinople. The barbarians have been active in destruction. The Christian Church has emerged triumphant. Then history presents on the scene a character who suggests in many ways the virtues of the great Romans in the days of the republic. Every opportunity is given Gibbon for contrasting the present scene with the greatness of the past. That he heightens the comparison is seen in the very first sentence with which he undertakes his narrative: 'While the Romans languished under the ignominious tyranny of eunuchs and bishops, the praises of Julian were repeated with transport in every part of the empire, except in the palace of Constantius.'[26] And the study of Julian's reign and character is concluded with one of the finest tributes Gibbon pays to any one of the characters in the whole length of his history.

> The remains of Julian were interred at Tarsus in Cilicia; but his stately tomb which arose in that city, on the banks of the cold and limpid Cydnus, was displeasing to the faithful friends, who loved and revered the memory of that extraordinary man. The philosopher expressed a very reasonable wish that the disciple of Plato might have reposed amidst the groves of the academy: while the soldiers exclaimed

[26] ii. 396.

in bolder accents that the ashes of Julian should have mingled with those of Caesar, in the field of Mars, and among the ancient monuments of Roman virtue. The history of princes does not very frequently renew the example of a similar competition.[27]

Julian is not the hero of *The Decline and Fall*; on the contrary, Gibbon is keenly aware of the faults of this emperor. But history has afforded an opportunity, which Gibbon seizes, to clarify all the elements of his narrative in the story of one memorable reign. The pagans dated their misfortunes from the fall of Julian, for his life was dedicated in peace and war to resisting the decline of Roman greatness. He fought the growing power of Christianity, and in a career of military glory he tried to equal Caesar and Alexander. His reign, which lasted only one year and seven months (A.D. December 361 to June 363), occupies three of Gibbon's most stirring chapters. The events were not important enough to justify such emphasis; Julian's importance in *The Decline and Fall* is determined on other grounds. He was killed while on his Persian expedition; he is succeeded by Jovian, whose feeble efforts can extricate the Roman legions only by an ignominious treaty. Gibbon pauses on this transaction: 'Sapor enjoyed the glory and the fruits of his victory; and this ignominious peace has justly been considered as a memorable aera in the decline and fall of the Roman empire. The predecessors of Jovian had sometimes relinquished the dominion of distant and unprofitable provinces; but, since the foundation of the city, the genius of Rome, the god Terminus, who guarded the boundaries of the republic, had never retired before the sword of a victorious enemy.'[28] But of greater importance to Gibbon is the fact that in the burial of Julian part of the great spirit of Rome is interred.

The same careful attention to form, order, and design seen in these twenty chapters will be found in Gibbon's management of all the larger strands of his work. His suspension of one narrative for the introduction of another and then his fusion of the two with other elements of his history is a common, but important, technique. It permits him to clarify the relationship of the parts, to employ shifting emphasis, and to derive from contrast a degree of illumination otherwise unobtainable. At the sacrifice of chrono-

[27] ii. 529–30.

[28] ii. 527.

logy, Gibbon achieves a vast amount of control over his material, and he is able to produce with far more precision exactly the effect he desires.

I should like to conclude this discussion of the larger elements of *The Decline and Fall* with the observation that history presented to Gibbon, as it does to any other historian, a great mass of raw material. The first shaping concept which he imposed on it was the coherence of the fall of a great empire. Beyond that, a series of subordinate concepts grew and developed as he prosecuted his studies and discovered the causes of the great events he records. Ingenuity can suggest to anyone numerous alternative ways of handling the same material, but the exercise will serve only to show the towering intellectual strength and energy required of Gibbon to bring into harmonious relation and clear patterns such a gigantic mass of confused and disparate material. The prominent features of *The Decline and Fall*, the organizing plan, its form as an epideictic oration, the division of its parts, the special emphases, did not come ready made. The raw, largely uninterpreted facts were there, and the efforts of preceding scholars like Tillemont were enormously helpful; but Gibbon alone determined the shape and pattern of his work. It is not so much the fact that one man was able to assimilate such a great quantity of detail that impresses us. It is rather the power of the mind that reduced this huge mass to order and coherence. Horace Walpole was delighted that he almost tricked Gibbon into making the boast that this vast amount of material had never before been put together so well. Yet Gibbon was fully entitled to make such a claim, nor has there been since *The Decline and Fall* any similar historical achievement.

IV · NARRATIVE

In describing the literature of the Arabians, Gibbon uses a phrase which might characterize his own efforts in *The Decline and Fall.* 'Their more elaborate compositions', he says, 'were addressed with energy and effect to the minds of their hearers'; and it is to the *minds* of his audience that Gibbon addresses his memorial oration. One should not come to Gibbon, as one does to Froude, Carlyle, or Michelet, for an imaginative re-creation of the past which the reader may experience vicariously. Gibbon insists on judgement and evaluation. The reader's emotions are engaged in many ways, but the degree and quality of the response are always carefully controlled. The orator raises the correct pitch of passion in the breasts of his audience, inflaming or depressing the spirit as the case may be, always moving it in the direction he desires. Gibbon would not, and perhaps could not, have written the glowing sentence of Michelet: 'I, who have excuses for so many things, regrets for so many diverse ages, I for whom all life is precious and who feel all humanity is my family and my blood, I move across history like the Greek actor who, when playing Electra, bore the funeral urn of his son.'[1] The human pageant in Gibbon's history is awesome, and there is a tragic awareness as he pursues the ruin of Rome; but the very essence of his art consists in gathering and directing into instructive channels the passions raised by the spectacle. His humanism rests less on compassion for erring humanity than on faith in the potential of human reason and in the instructive value of history. His attitude towards his work can be seen clearly in a passage which contrasts sharply with my quotation from Michelet. After a series of particularly despicable events, Gibbon reflects:

> A being of the nature of man, endowed with the same faculties, but with a longer measure of existence, would cast down a smile of pity and contempt on the crimes and follies of human ambition, so eager, in a narrow span, to grasp at a precarious and short-lived enjoyment.

[1] Quoted by Emery Neff, *The Poetry of History* (New York, 1947), p. 149.

It is thus that the experience of history exalts and enlarges the horizon of our intellectual view. In a composition of some days, in a perusal of some hours, six hundred years have rolled away, and the duration of a life or reign is contracted to a fleeting moment; . . . and our immortal reason survives and disdains the sixty phantoms of kings, who have passed before our eyes and faintly dwell on our remembrance.[2]

There is drama in Gibbon, and quite often a lively immediacy in his representations, but the ultimate appeal of everything he writes is to the 'immortal reason' which he saw triumphant in his own age. Passion is enlisted in the support of judgement; sympathy rather than empathy is demanded from the reader; and the historian who wishes to make a judicial interpretation of events arouses or soothes the hearts of his audience that he may lead them to share his understandings. It is the purpose of this chapter to examine some of Gibbon's more important techniques of narrative that we may perceive the manner in which he controls and directs the responses of his readers. Having already discussed such large considerations as point of view, tone, and management of the major themes, I should now like to describe the details of Gibbon's art.

In the fourteen centuries covered by *The Decline and Fall*, battles comprise a large portion of the whole. In the course of his history the most voracious appetite for war will have been satiated, Gibbons says, and in my discussion of narrative techniques his handling of these violent scenes will supply a suitable introduction. A representative example is found in the great battle of Mursa, which terminated the civil war between Constantius and Magnentius. The forces of the empire, says Gibbon, were consumed on this field.

The preparations for the battle generate suspense and prepare the reader for great actions: 'The approaching contest with Magnentius was of a more serious and bloody kind. The tyrant advanced by rapid marches to encounter Constantius, at the head of a numerous army, composed of Gauls and Spaniards, of Franks and Saxons. . . .'[3] With effective economy, Gibbon describes the

[2] *The History of the Decline and Fall of the Roman Empire*, J. B. Bury, ed. (7 vols., London, 1896–1900), v. 242–3.

[3] ii. 238.

scene of the action and the speedy initiation of hostilities: 'The fertile plains of the lower Pannonia, between the Drave, the Save, and the Danube, presented a spacious theatre; and the operations of the civil war were protracted during the summer months by the skill or timidity of the combatants.' The sparring of the generals is then described in a way which gives the reader considerable penetration into their different states of mind. Constantius was timid, Magnentius was aggressive. Constantius undertook negotiations for peace, but these efforts were fruitless, and Gibbon quickly brings us to the city of Mursa, which had been attacked by Magnentius towards the end of September. The scene is narrowed to a smaller area. 'The city of Mursa, or Essek, celebrated in modern times for a bridge of boats five miles in length over the river Drave and the adjacent morasses, has been always considered as a place of importance in the wars of Hungary. Magnentius, directing his march towards Mursa, set fire to the gates, and, by a sudden assault, had almost scaled the walls of the town.' The information about the bridge of boats may seem gratuitous in this context until we remember the overall point of view of the history. Gibbon and his audience look back together over the centuries into the darkness of the past.

The sudden arrival of Constantius on the scene breaks up the siege, and Gibbon prepares his readers for the battle itself. The terrain is described, a naked and level plain; the lines of battle are drawn; and he singles out the one significant feature for emphasis: the left side of the army of Constantius extended far beyond the right flank of Magnentius. This fact is decisive in the subsequent action. The lull before the battle is suggested by the statement: 'The troops on both sides remained under arms in anxious expectation during the greatest part of the morning'; but we are suddenly and forcibly reminded of the larger perspective and significance of the occasion by the last part of the same sentence: 'and the son of Constantine, after animating his soldiers by an eloquent speech, retired into a church at a safe distance from the field of battle, and committed to his generals the conduct of this decisive day'. The contempt for Constantius which arises from the contrast of his actions with those of his brave and anxious troops renders all the more painful the following narrative in which so many lives are lost that he might ascend and abuse the throne.

I quote Gibbon's description of the battle in full. The generals of Constantius, he writes,

> wisely began the action upon the left; and, advancing their whole wing of cavalry in an oblique line, they suddenly wheeled it on the right flank of the enemy, which was unprepared to resist the impetuosity of their charge. But the Romans of the West soon rallied, by the habits of discipline; and the Barbarians of Germany supported the renown of their national bravery. The engagement soon became general; was maintained with various and singular turns of fortune; and scarcely ended with the darkness of night. The signal victory which Constantius obtained is attributed to the arms of his cavalry. His cuirassiers are described as so many massy statues of steel, glittering with their scaly armour, and breaking with their ponderous lances the firm array of the Gallic legions. As soon as the legions gave way, the lighter and more active squadrons of the second line rode sword in hand into the intervals, and completed the disorder. In the meanwhile, the huge bodies of the Germans were exposed almost naked to the dexterity of the oriental archers; and whole troops of those Barbarians were urged by anguish and despair to precipitate themselves into the broad and rapid stream of the Drave. The number of the slain was computed at fifty-four thousand men, and the slaughter of the conquerors was more considerable than that of the vanquished; a circumstance which proves the obstinacy of the contest, and justifies the observation of an ancient writer that the forces of the empire were consumed in the fatal battle of Mursa, by the loss of a veteran army, sufficient to defend the frontiers or to add new triumphs to the glory of Rome.

Perhaps the most extraordinary feature of this passage is the degree to which the reader becomes involved in the conflict without at the same time ever losing perspective on the whole. The narrative begins with the general movement of armies and ends with the significance of the battle to the fortunes of the empire; but as the engagement itself becomes more general, so reader participation increases. The mention of Constantius's victory halfway through the paragraph releases the suspense and allows the reader to visualize the details of the action. The whole action is viewed by a sensitive witness of the scene, and his thoughts, as he surveys the carnage of the day, lead us back to the importance of the loss in the history of Rome. When we reflect on the appeal which has been made to our senses and through them to our imagination, it will be apparent that we have not heard the shouts or the cries; we have not tasted the dust on our tongues, nor felt the heat of the sun or the dreadful fatigue. But we are aware of ponderous lances, glittering steel, pierced bodies, and 54,000 corpses. Characteristically, Gibbon has selected several distinguishing features and let them imply the rest.

In this brief narrative there is something of a static quality; action is caught at its most violent moment and held. The ponderous lances are seen just as they break the firm array of the legions; huge bodies are exposed to the dexterity of the archers. Although there has been considerable movement and violence, the artist is not so much interested in imitating the movement as he is in extracting its quality. The break in chronology is the key; having indicated the outcome of the battle quite early in the paragraph, Gibbon then gathers the characterizing details and displays them in preparation for the final assessment of the action. In short, we can say that in reading Gibbon's narrative, we have experienced the suspense, we have been given a suitable context, we have shared in the excitement, we have been brought close enough to the field to see the violence, to perceive the quality of the action, and yet finally, we discover that the whole account has really been addressed to our minds, as we share the judgement of the ancient writer that this battle was a major calamity for the empire.

If one reflects on the thousands of battles and skirmishes covered in the long history of *The Decline and Fall,* one will understand Gibbon's need to discriminate the characteristic features of each, and to employ them in the most telling way. Consider, for example, the description of Julian's battle with the Persians which followed immediately after his successful crossing of the Tigris. All the glory and power of the legions are caught in a few lines, and yet we see their actions through the intervening darkness of centuries which covers all but the most striking details.

As soon as they possessed a more equal field, Julian, who with his light infantry, had led the attack, darted through the ranks a skilful and experienced eye: his bravest soldiers, according to the precepts of Homer, were distributed in the front and rear; and all the trumpets of the imperial army sounded to battle. The Romans, after sending up a military shout, advanced in measured steps to the animating notes of martial music; launched their formidable javelines; and rushed forwards, with drawn swords, to deprive the Barbarians, by closer onset, of the advantage of their missile weapons. The whole engagement lasted above twelve hours; till the gradual retreat of the Persians was changed to disorderly flight. . . .[4]

And so it is with a host of other actions. In the crusaders' attack on Constantinople, the lines appear, 'they approached the walls; and a desperate conflict of swords, spears, and battle-axes was fought on the trembling bridges that grappled the floating to the stable batteries'.[5] And in a description of troops of Belisarius, when they were hard pressed by the Persians, we find the comments: 'They turned their backs to the Euphrates, and their faces to the enemy; innumerable arrows glanced without effect from the compact and shelving order of their bucklers; and an impenetrable line of pikes was opposed to the repeated assaults of the Persian cavalry; and after a resistance of many hours, the remaining troops were skilfully embarked under the shadow of the night.'[6] In all of these passages there is movement, of course, but in capturing the key features of the action, Gibbon has confined it and arrested it in its moment of greatest vitality, stripped of superfluous detail. We do not see the terrain nor do we know the time of day when Julian fought the particular battle under consideration. In the attack on Constantinople we see in the foreground a conflict of weapons—swords, spears, and battle-axes, and the reader fills in the human faces and cries which are left in the shadowy background. In the next example we see a 'compact and shelving order of bucklers' and 'an impenetrable line of pikes'.

If one searches among the other art forms for a parallel to Gibbon's manner of visualizing the details of these actions, one finds that the Roman bas-relief or frieze, which adorned the triumphal arches and public buildings of the capital, affords a profitable comparison. The most memorable features of a campaign were selected from a host of other details and boldly sculptured to commemorate the achievements of the various conquerors. One such monument in particular comes to mind, and that is the magnificent column erected by Trajan. Gibbon, we know, was deeply impressed by it on his first visit to Rome. He wrote to his father: 'I was this morning upon the top of Trajan's

[4] ii. 505. [5] vi. 404. [6] iv. 275.

pillar. I shall not attempt a description of it. Only figure to yourself a column 140 foot high of the purest white marble composed only of about 30 blocks and wrought into bas-reliefs with ... much taste and delicacy. . . .'[7] It would be going too far to claim that he consciously sought to achieve with his narrative the effect of a frieze, even though we gather from numerous passages in *The Decline and Fall* that he was greatly interested in sculpture. It is enough simply to point out that Gibbon's narrative produces in the mind of the reader a similar effect. The significant movements are caught at the moment of their greatest intensity and held up to the judgement of the reader. The quality of the action is determined by judicious selection of detail. Quite often the accounts of battles suggest Matthew Arnold's lines:

> And we are here as on a darkling plain
> Swept with confused alarms of struggle and flight,
> Where ignorant armies clash by night.

Yet, in every case, the dominant features of an action emerge from the surrounding darkness with the clarity which characterizes all of Gibbon's writing. The ravages of time have obliterated all but the most distinguishing features; yet tension results from the degree of immediacy with which they are seen.

From these examples it is apparent that Gibbon's appeal to the minds of his audience rests on the amount of commentary he has been able to work into his descriptions of actions. In the account of the battle of Mursa, the most highly charged and connotative details were used as characterizing features, but the reader's response to them is carefully controlled by the context in which they occur or by the implications Gibbon is able to derive from them. Narrative commentary is such an important part of Gibbon's composition that an example of it drawn from a different kind of action will be appropriate. In the ecclesiastical conflict over the worship of images, Leo the Iconoclast, one of the Byzantine emperors, declared himself opposed to such practices as a revival of paganism. He met with considerable opposition. Gibbon draws the conflict in terms suited to the most memorable of actions.

[7] *The Letters of Edward Gibbon*, J. E. Norton, ed. (3 vols., New York, 1956), i. 184.

The scandal of an abstract heresy can be only proclaimed to the people by the blast of the ecclesiastical trumpet; but the most ignorant can perceive, the most torpid must feel, the profanation and downfall of their visible deities. The first hostilities of Leo were directed against a lofty Christ on the vestibule, and above the gate, of the palace. A ladder had been planted for the assault, but it was furiously shaken by a crowd of zealots and women; they beheld, with pious transport, the ministers of sacrilege tumbling from on high and dashed against the pavement; and the honours of the ancient martyrs were prostituted to these criminals, who justly suffered for murder and rebellion.[8]

From the dignity of tone with which this paragraph is invested, something of the mock-heroic spirit emerges. One might note how the ridiculous in the paragraph gives way to indignation and outrage just about the time we get to the phrase, 'pious transport'. Gibbon never lets his reader forget that though the land might seem to be Lilliput, the figures are sadly enough life-size. Another important feature is found in the connotative details. Ecclesiastical trumpets blast; the ladder is furiously shaken; the women and zealots are criminals. We are not bothered with the information that several men had climbed the ladder; we only see them tumble; we are not informed how the women and zealots were quelled, nor do we know the form of their punishment. We are asked to regard them as criminals who suffer justly for murder; we infer that they were killed, because they are associated with the early martyrs, but this comparison gives us a chance to measure the extent to which, in Gibbon's mind, the Church had degenerated. This thought reflects back on the ecclesiastical trumpets, the blasting of which might at first have amused us. In short, we have to take from the paragraph exactly what Gibbon wants us to take, and in precisely the way he wants us to take it. He has related an action and commented upon it simultaneously.

These examples illustrate a major quality of Gibbon's prose, and that is its *solidity*. I use this term with Middleton Murry's definition in mind: 'complete economy, complete precision, and over and above these things it is understood to imply that the piece of writing has been completely ejected from the author's mind'.[9]

[8] *The Decline and Fall*, v. 253–4.

[9] *The Problem of Style* (London, 1922), p. 90.

Gibbon's interest in clarity and his desire to obtain full intellectual apprehension are illustrated by other practices. Very frequently, he will introduce an action by a discussion of the principles involved. In this way he is able to place the narrative in precisely the intellectual and emotional climate most appropriate to it. The crusades, for example, illustrate a savage fanaticism, and the entire narrative is conducted in the light of this prefatory remark. A discussion of the lasting victory which Christianity obtained after the death of Julian, and during the reign of Jovian, is preceded by the observation: 'The slightest force, when it is applied to assist and guide the natural descent of its object, operates with irresistible weight; and Jovian had the good fortune to embrace the religious opinions which were supported by the spirit of the times and the zeal and numbers of the most powerful sect.'[10] The analogy drawn from natural law is concerned with the fall of an object, and it gives us at the same time the reason for the triumph of Christianity in the reign of Jovian and Gibbon's opinion of this victory. Sometimes he will use a literary comparison to differentiate the specific actions with which he is occupied from others which the reader may recall:

> When Tacitus describes the deaths of the innocent and illustrious Romans, who were sacrificed to the cruelty of the first Caesars, the art of the historian, or the merit of the sufferers, excite in our breasts the most lively sensations of terror, of admiration, and of pity. The coarse and undistinguishing pencil of Ammianus has delineated his bloody figures with tedious and disgusting accuracy. But, as our attention is no longer engaged by the contrast of freedom and servitude, of recent greatness and of actual misery, we should turn with horror from the frequent executions which disgraced, both at Rome and Antioch, the reign of the two brothers [i.e. Valens and Valentinian].[11]

Gibbon's interest, which is central to all his writing, and perhaps one of his strongest merits, lies in the art of definition. As against the 'coarse and undistinguishing pencil', he sought and achieved an unusual precision in discriminating and setting limits. His prose is a continuous 'raid on the inarticulate'.

The extraordinary effects which he achieves from the use of parallel situations, literary and historical, and from his emphasis

[10] iii. 3. [11] iii. 19.

on general or fundamental principles, can be seen in a final example which is the beginning of an extended comparison of the sack of Rome by the Goths with both earlier and later pillages of the city. The importance of this event, the first conquest of the city since Rome had emerged to empire, justifies Gibbon's pause to observe:

> There exists in human nature a strong propensity to depreciate the advantages, and to magnify the evils, of the present times. Yet, when the first emotions had subsided, and a fair estimate was made of the real damage, the more learned and judicious contemporaries were forced to confess that infant Rome had formerly received more essential injury from the Gauls than she had sustained from the Goths in her declining age. The experience of eleven centuries had enabled posterity to produce a much more singular parallel; and to affirm with confidence that the ravages of the Barbarians, whom Alaric had led from the banks of the Danube, were less destructive than the hostilities exercised by the troops of Charles the Fifth, a Catholic prince, who styled himself Emperor of the Romans.[12]

An outgrowth of Gibbon's interest in precise definition is his desire to discover the exact motivating forces of the action. His search sometimes takes him geographically far away from the immediate theatre or to situations not immediately concerned with the chronology of his narrative. In considering the invasions of the Huns and Goths during the fourth century, for example, a digression on the manners of pastoral nations is required, because 'The original principle of motion was concealed in the remote countries of the North'.[13] On important matters, such as the cause for barbarian invasions, or the crusades, or Constantine's conversion to Christianity, the study of motivation is full and often long. It is never dry or tedious. When the motives of the actors are accessible to the historian, they are applied to our understanding of the action with skill and power. But 'the springs of action' are not always visible. Motives frequently appear ambiguous and sometimes elude the penetration of the writer. In cases where he cannot pronounce with assurance, he eliminates some of the obscurity by assigning alternative motives. 'The pride or the policy', 'the superstition or the greed', 'the piety or the avarice', are characteristic phrases used in such situations; and sometimes

[12] iii. 328. [13] iii. 70.

motives that seem on first glance to be mutually exclusive are yoked together: for example, 'the courage or the fear'. To clarify the dark and the obscure is his intention, and even though the frequent use of alternatives sometimes appears a stylistic vice, it is saved from being so by the extra release of energy in the representation of a single action with contrasting determinants. Moreover, the reader is continually reminded of the fallibility of human nature. Sometimes the first motive is the one a character shows to the world, and the second the one he shows to himself.

It is characteristic of Gibbon that in his efforts to eliminate vagueness from his writing he should go so far as to atomize the human personality in the same fashion that he dissects the totality of events to emphasize significant features. Sometimes we find the simple personification of passions: 'After the second victory of Belisarius, envy again whispered, Justinian listened, and the hero was recalled.'[14] But more commonly, the passion, virtue, or vice is the acting agent. It is the *pride* of Constantius which condescends to solicit a treaty. Not Marcellinus, but 'the friendship of Marcellinus' supplies money and riches for bribery. Not Gregory, but the 'magnanimous spirit of Gregory' embraces a particular design. It is the 'honour and interest of Theodoric' which are wounded by the disgrace of a friend, and it is the 'emulation of valour' (the men motivated by it are not mentioned) which follows the example of a hero. The 'hopes of fortune' are said to have depopulated part of a country, and we have already noticed that in the battle of Mursa the Germans were exposed to the 'dexterity' of the archers, and only by implication to their arrows. Quite often such atomization is merely an instrument of grace and variety; it always has the effect of placing the emphasis precisely where Gibbon wishes it. In the first terrible sack of Rome by the Goths, we get the following description:

> In the pillage of Rome, a just preference was given to gold and jewels, which contain the greatest value in the smallest compass and weight; but, after these portable riches had been removed by the more diligent robbers, the palaces of Rome were rudely stripped of their splendid and costly furniture. The sideboards of massy plate, and the variegated wardrobes of silk and purple were irregularly piled in the waggons that always followed the march of a Gothic army. The

[14] iv. 332.

most exquisite works of art were roughly handled or wantonly destroyed: many a statue was melted for the sake of the precious materials; and many a vase, in the division of the spoil, was shivered into fragments by the stroke of a battle-axe.[15]

The use of the passive voice in this passage has a peculiar and valuable effect. These things are acted upon by an implied agent which piles in wagons, handles roughly, destroys wantonly, and shivers vases into fragments. Our mind's eye sees a horde of semi-naked, shouting savages, some of whom, more diligent than the others, are explicitly mentioned. Far more important to Gibbon, however, is the principle of their motivation. He introduces the passage with the remark that 'avarice is an insatiate and universal passion', and it is the passion of avarice which performs the action here. The features of the individual men possessed by it are obliterated, and we do not even see the hand that wields the battle-axe. Among the ancients, some passions were considered so powerful that they were derived from the gods themselves, and Phaedra could declare with conviction that it was a god driving her to the mad love for Hippolytus. Gibbon is far from assigning such actions to the gods, but his remark that the historian is aided by 'the knowledge of human nature, and of the sure operation of its fierce and unrestrained passions', may help to illustrate his art. By using the passive voice, he has given us a clear and steady look at the monstrous passion which animates all the barbarians and obliterates every trace of individuality. The real subject of the selection is the effects of avarice on Roman riches. The paragraph continues with the effects of violence on Roman buildings. It is Rome that is suffering; the individual actors, conquerors and conquered, are grouped and classified as they fit into this larger picture. Misers are tortured, virgins raped, matrons, 'from want of youth or beauty', are spared, and slaves retaliate their injuries on their masters.

Moreover, Gibbon's skilful dissection of his material is accomplished without sacrificing a vital, dynamic narrative. The opening narrative of the sack of Rome begins characteristically with a single, specific detail which is immediately generalized. 'At the hour of midnight, the Salarian gate was silently opened, and the inhabitants were awakened by the tremendous sound of the

[15] iii. 325.

Gothic trumpet. Eleven hundred and sixty-three years after the foundation of Rome, the Imperial city, which had subdued and civilized so considerable a part of mankind, was delivered to the licentious fury of the tribes of Germany and Scythia.'[16] In the first sentence we share the horror of the Romans who hear in the darkness of the night 'the tremendous sound of the Gothic trumpet'. In the next sentence we have the long view of the duration of the imperial city and the value of its contribution to civilization, a view which is gradually brought back to the licentious fury of the barbarians. The mass of violent actions which follows is sometimes handled with the large, general view we have discussed: individuals are lost in the mob violence of tyrannical passions: avarice, lust, and rapine dominate the scene. Then Gibbon produces an anecdote, carefully selected to illustrate typical actions either by direct parallel or contrast. Throughout the description the tension between the specific and the general, between the immediate and the distant, between the part and the whole is carefully maintained. In bridging the gap between them we take away much more than would otherwise be possible. In a more immediate representation we would lose the perspective of the whole; if we had only the larger perspective, we would miss the flavour and quality of the action. Gibbon here, as in most other sections of his narrative, places his reader on middle ground from which he can extend his understanding to each of the parts while maintaining the larger vision. The body is dissected, but it is still alive and entire. Horace Walpole, in discussing Dr. Robertson, puts the matter very well in respect to Gibbon: 'As Dr. Robertson has not the genius, penetration, sagacity, and art of Mr. Gibbon, he cannot melt his materials together and make them elucidate, and even improve and produce, new discoveries; in short, he cannot, like Mr. Gibbon, make an *original* picture with some bits of Mosaic.'[17]

I have mentioned Gibbon's use of anecdote to illustrate typical actions, and this practice deserves more comment. His sources supplied him often with eye-witness accounts of the events he describes as well as speeches and letters of the participants. His

[16] iii. 321–2.

[17] Quoted by G. B. Hill, ed., *The Memoirs of Edward Gibbon* (New York, 1900), p. 297.

narrative is rendered more concrete and immediate by his frequent use of these materials. Often they are employed to assist when other information is lacking, or they are used simply as illustrative features. He improves his narrative of the dismal hostilities in the ninth century by this scheme: 'Among the hostilities of the Arabs, the Franks, and the Greeks, in southern Italy, I shall select two or three anecdotes expressive of their national manners.'[18] Two of them are bawdy, lusty tales, and the third is a story of heroic virtue. All three help rescue from tedium a narrative full of calamities and woes.

Another element of Gibbon's narrative which deserves consideration is the matter of descriptive background and geographic setting, and the extent to which they are worked into the story. In his description of the battle of Mursa, after placing that city on the map for his readers and pointing out its importance in modern times, he simply adds that it was situated on a naked plain. It is generally true that landscape and details of natural setting enter infrequently into Gibbon's pages except when they have some bearing on the action, or when the importance of the place justifies a full account of its location. His landscapes are always peopled, and even the description of a scene of desolation and ruin is animated by the presence of a lonely traveller: 'The ruins of Carthage have perished; and the place might be unknown, if some broken arches of an aqueduct did not guide the footsteps of the inquisitive traveller.'[19] The wastes of the Sahara, when they are visited by Gibbon, are discovered to contain human life and action: '... a rustic horn or trumpet, the signal of devotion, twice interrupted the vast silence of the desert.'[20] Scenes of emptiness and solitude are vitalized by memory of past activity: '... a vast and gloomy silence prevailed in that venerable dome, which had so often smoked with a cloud of incense, blazed with innumerable lights, and resounded with the voice of prayer and thanksgiving.'[21] And when Gibbon indulges in a full descriptive passage, it is almost always concerned with a great spectacle or pageant, vibrant with human life and action.

Landscape and background, when they do enter, are usually suggested by Gibbon's selection of generalized detail which is used

[18] *The Decline and Fall*, vi. 171.
[19] v. 469.
[20] iv. 71.
[21] vii. 177.

as part of the narrative commentary. When the army of Julian had taken the Persian city of Maogamalcha, Gibbon continues: 'The neighbourhood of the capital of Persia was adorned with three stately palaces, laboriously enriched with every production that could gratify the luxury and pride of an Eastern monarch. The pleasant situation of the gardens along the banks of the Tigris was improved, according to the Persian taste, by the symmetry of flowers, fountains, and shady walks: and spacious parks were enclosed for the reception of bears, lions, and wild boars, which were maintained at a considerable expense for the pleasure of the royal chace.'[22] The soldiers of Julian, by his command, destroy the palaces, gardens, and animals, and the fleeting glimpse of oriental luxury gives way to the thought that Julian on this occasion showed himself ignorant of the laws of civility between hostile princes. All we see of the city of Maogamalcha itself before it is razed is what a soldier might see: sixteen large towers, a deep ditch, and two strong, solid walls of brick and bitumen.

Earlier in the narrative, the country in which the Romans find themselves had been described as fruitful and pleasant, and plentifully supplied with water and forage. But we get no farther in visualizing the plains of Assyria and the nature of her cities than the view presented in the paragraph which introduces the narrative. The geographical limits, the climate, and the soil of Assyria are briefly described. Then Gibbon continues:

> To the soil and climate of Assyria nature had denied some of her choicest gifts, the vine, the olive, and the fig tree; but the food which supports the life of man, and particularly wheat and barley, were produced with inexhaustible fertility; and the husbandman who committed his seed to the earth was frequently rewarded with an increase of two, or even of three, hundred. The face of the country was interspersed with groves of innumerable palm-trees; and the diligent natives celebrated, either in verse or prose, the three hundred and sixty uses to which the trunk, the branches, the leaves, the juice, and the fruit, were skilfully applied. Several manufactures, especially those of leather and linen, employed the industry of a numerous people. . . .[23]

With these details and several others, Gibbon fills in the back-

[22] ii. 499. [23] ii. 496.

ground for the battles of Julian in the country of the Persians; and here again we find him occupying a middle ground between the immediate and the general. We come so close that we can feel 'the soft and yielding' texture of the soil, and we draw so far back that we may contemplate the 360 uses of the palm-tree.

On such important matters as the site of Constantinople, Gibbon's descriptive powers are more fully exercised. The thesis of his description is stated at the end: 'The prospect of beauty, of safety, and of wealth, united in a single spot, was sufficient to justify the choice of Constantine.'[24] In addition to demonstrating his thesis, however, he parades a host of memories which a lover of classical literature associates with the general area. We view the Bosphorus and Propontis with the eye of a modern traveller and see a 'rich prospect of vineyards, of gardens, and of plentiful harvests'. Or we are given a glimpse of the Hellespont when 'Xerxes imposed a stupendous bridge of boats, for the purpose of transporting into Europe an hundred and seventy myriads of barbarians'. More interestingly, Gibbon pauses on the question of why Homer and Orpheus called the Hellespont broad; and his imagination wanders back to the time of Troy: 'our ideas of greatness are of a relative nature: the traveller, and especially the poet, who sailed along the Hellespont, who pursued the windings of the stream, and contemplated the rural scenery, which appeared on every side to terminate the prospect, insensibly lost the remembrance of the sea; and his fancy painted those celebrated straits with all the attributes of a mighty river flowing with a swift current, in the midst of a woody and inland country, and at length, through a wide mouth, discharging itself into the Aegean or Archipelago.'[25] This close look through the eyes of Homer has been prefaced by the view of the present-day sailor; or, indeed, the sailor of any age: 'Those who steer their westward course through the middle of the Propontis may at once descry the high lands of Thrace and Bithynia, and never lose sight of the lofty summit of Mount Olympus, covered with eternal snows.' Side by side in this splendid section we find the points of view of all ages; modern castles are built on the sites of ancient temples, which in their turn have been constructed on the ruined altars of the most primitive worshippers. The depth of the harbours, the precise

[24] ii. 147. [25] ii. 145.

measurements of the straits, the fish which are caught in the Propontis, the temperature of the air—these matters are carefully introduced beside the recollection of the imperial residence of Diocletian, the camps of Agamemnon and Achilles, the voyage of the Argonauts, and Phineus's palace, infested by the obscene harpies. So many centuries are suddenly compressed into Gibbon's description that the mind is dazzled: it is the unchanging spirit and character of the place which he has sought to capture. If D. H. Lawrence had been writing the description or commenting upon it, he would have observed that this was one of the 'quick' spots of the earth. Gibbon is content to observe with classical restraint that the advantageous position of Constantinople 'appears to have been formed by Nature for the centre and capital of a great monarchy'.

Constantinople was constructed in a period of decline, and from its very conception until its final capture by the Turks, the city is characterized by the ebbing of vital powers. Only in the city of Rome does Gibbon find a vital principle, the genius of the city, which survives all catastrophe and animates throughout the long period of the history, indeed, throughout twenty-four centuries, the changing temper of the populace. But the characters of important cities, Antioch, Alexandria, Constantinople, do concern Gibbon, and in describing the foundation of the new seat of empire the essential and unchanging nature of its location provides the context for its construction: it is a city born in a state of premature and permanent decay. 'Constantine soon discovered that, in the decline of the arts, the skill as well as numbers of his architects bore a very unequal proportion to the greatness of his designs.'[26] The city must perforce be decorated with the great works of antiquity, for to 'revive the genius of Phidias and Lysippus surpassed indeed the power of a Roman emperor'. And the comment of the historian Cedrenus may be taken as expressing Gibbon's sentiments: 'nothing seemed wanting except the souls of the illustrious men whom those admirable monuments were intended to represent'.[27] We discover now that the memories of gods and heroes which have been introduced into Gibbon's description of the Bosphorus, Propontis, and Hellespont have not been simply gratuitous, an extra loading of each rift with ore. Rather they are designed to contrast with the residents of the new city, and

[26] ii. 151.

[27] Ibid.

their use affords us another illustration of Gibbon's genius for perspective.

Any discussion of Gibbon's descriptive style should not leave the impression that he is incapable of creating sensuous, even sensual beauty. The contrary is true. The luxury, the pomp and richness of the pageantry which fills the pages of *The Decline and Fall* afford him considerable exercise in painting verbal pictures. In his representation of one landscape, for example, we find a passage which is suggestive of Spenser's Bower of Acrasia, and, except for the profane delights, is reminiscent in many ways of Milton's Paradise. Gibbon describes the grove of Daphne, about five miles from Antioch:

> The temple and the village were deeply bosomed in a thick grove of laurels and cypresses, which reached as far as a circumference of ten miles, and formed in the most sultry summers a cool and impenetrable shade. A thousand streams of purest water, issuing from every hill, preserved the verdure of the earth and the temperature of the air; the senses were gratified with harmonious sounds and aromatic odours; and the peaceful grove was consecrated to health and joy, to luxury and love. The vigorous youth pursued, like Apollo, the object of his desires; and the blushing maid was warned, by the fate of Daphne, to shun the folly of unseasonable coyness. The soldier and the philosopher wisely avoided the temptation of this sensual paradise; where pleasure, assuming the character of religion, imperceptibly dissolved the firmness of manly virtue.[28]

In the characteristic neo-classical manner, the scene is not distinguished by individualized detail: the 'streaks of the tulip' are not counted. We see instead, 'impenetrable shade', 'a thousand streams', 'the verdure of the earth', 'the vigorous youth', and 'the blushing maid'; we hear 'harmonious sounds' and smell 'aromatic odours'. Readers of *Paradise Lost* may wish to place Milton's description of Paradise in Book Four with its 'unpierced shade' and 'crisped brooks' beside Gibbon's similar phrases. The visual art of the two writers is very close in these passages. Both descriptions are constructed in a similar fashion with first the general picture (compare Milton's 'A happy rural seat of various view'), and then the enumeration of characteristic details. Milton draws from mythology stories of maidens loved by gods.

[28] ii. 466–7.

Not that fair field
Of Enna, where Proserpine gathering flow'rs,
Herself a fairer flow'r, by gloomy Dis
Was gathered, which cost Ceres all that pain
To seek her through the world; not that sweet grove
Of Daphne by Orontes, and the inspired
Castalian spring, might with this Paradise
Of Eden strive. . . .[29]

And Gibbon, who also had indulged himself in the luxuries and warmth of pagan mythology, disengages himself from the scene by considering its effect on manly virtue. Both writers ornamented their works with the treasures of the classical age, which not only enrich but also increase the dimensions of the picture which the reader receives.

A final feature of Gibbon's narrative deserving special notice is his use of verbs. The orator seems to achieve almost personal control over the movements of armies. The Venetian fleet, carrying the crusaders to Constantinople, for example, is described at a distance, but not at so great a distance that the action is vague. 'As they *penetrated* through the Hellespont, the magnitude of their navy *was compressed* in a narrow channel; and the face of the waters *was darkened* with innumerable sails. They again *expanded* in the bason of the Propontis, and *traversed* that placid sea, till they *approached* the European shore. . . .'[30] The sense of massed power, seen here expanding and contracting, prepares the reader for the magnitude of the struggle to come. The movement is slow, ponderous, and threatening.

In Gibbon's description of the details of an action, a total calamity is sometimes divided, and the various parts are distributed to the proper verbs: 'Deprived of the only chief whom they could fear or esteem, the bands which he had led to victory were twice *broken* by the cavalry, *trampled* by the elephants, and *pierced* by the arrows of the barbarians. . . .'[31] Careful selection of verbs combined with variation of sentence length regulates exactly the speed of the following action. It gathers momentum to reach a climax precisely on the verb *pierced*. 'Some *were bathing* their huge limbs in the river; others *were combing* their

[29] Lines 268–75.
[30] vi. 391. Italics mine.
[31] v. 69. Italics mine.

long and flaxen hair; others again *were swallowing* large draughts of rich and delicious wine. On a sudden they *heard* the sound of the Roman trumpet; they *saw* the enemy in their camp. Astonishment *produced* disorder; disorder *was followed* by flight and dismay; and the confused multitude of the bravest warriors *was pierced* by the swords and javelins of the legionaries and auxiliaries.'[32] The large number of verbal nouns and adjectives which one finds in the sentences of Gibbon simply illustrates his interest in capturing and holding the vital in a position where it may be appraised. In the example just quoted, 'and' is the only word in the phrases 'Astonishment produced disorder; disorder was followed by flight and dismay', which does not have its roots struck deep in action.

Sometimes in a rapid narrative of obscure and unprofitable events, Gibbon will heap up his verbs and by this means inject some humour into what would otherwise be a tiresome account of the dismal activities so often met with in the long history. 'Besieging Rome by land and water, he thrice *entered* the gates as a barbarian conqueror; *profaned* the altars, *violated* the virgins, *pillaged* the merchants, *performed* his devotions at St. Peter's, and *left* a garrison in the castle of St. Angelo.'[33] As a final note on Gibbon's use of verbs, I might point out that even attitudes and opinions are moved with the same care and precision as great armies: 'By the imprudent conduct of the ministers of Honorius, the republic *lost* the assistance, and *deserved* the enmity, of thirty thousand of her bravest soldiers; and the weight of that formidable army, which alone might have determined the event of the war, *was transferred* from the scale of the Romans into that of the Goths.'[34]

The canvas of Gibbon teems with life, but the actions represented are always subjected to the control and discipline of the artist. The two great activities of his mind, dissection and analysis on the one hand, and fusion and creation on the other, are carried on concurrently. The simultaneous activity of taking apart and putting together makes his narrative a continual commentary. It is to his interest wherever possible to distinguish with precision the ingredients which make up the whole, or as he puts it in one

[32] iii. 33–34. Italics mine.

[33] vii. 286. Italics mine.

[34] iii. 286. Italics mine.

place, 'to ascertain the separate shares of accident, of fancy, of imposture, and of fiction'. As an artist, however, conducting a tremendous narrative, he must put together and create from the individual parts the living picture. Of one of his representations, he has commented in a footnote: 'In obedience to Jerom and Claudian, . . . I have mixed some darker colours in the mild representation of Zosimus, who wished to soften the calamities of Athens.'[35] And the comment illustrates part of the creative side of his mind. He measures precisely the degree of involvement he will permit his readers and the distance from which they are allowed to view the spectacle. Everywhere there is control, and beyond that a sense of completeness. Nothing that needs saying has been left unsaid. The focus is always on man and his activities, and the rest of the world is brought in only in so far as it bears on his destiny. With this fact in mind, we may now turn to a study of the individual actors in *The Decline and Fall.*

[35] iii. 243, n. 8.

V · CHARACTERS

> It was an ancient custom in the funerals, as well as in the triumphs, of the Romans, that the voice of praise should be corrected by that of satire and ridicule; and that, in the midst of the splendid pageants, which displayed the glory of the living or of the dead, their imperfections should not be concealed from the eyes of the world.[1]

In his widely read *Letters on the Study of History*, Lord Bolingbroke expressed a commonplace of eighteenth-century thought when he wrote: 'Man is the subject of every history; and to know him well, we must see him and consider him as history alone can present him to us, in every age, in every country, in every state.... History makes possible the knowledge of our species and of ourselves.'[2] Hume saw the study of history as an effort to discover the constant and universal principles of human nature. Gibbon half-seriously describes history as nothing but a record of the crimes and follies of mankind, but as a philosophic historian he undertook as his primary obligation the elucidation of the nature and destiny of man. Whether savage or civilized, noble or beastly, man in all of his capacities and in the tremendous variety of his existence is the object of primary attention. He is seen as the moulder and modifier of the great forces of history, just as he is often regarded as their product. The question of his origin, like the problem of the ultimate meaning of his existence, is left in the outer darkness which surrounds *The Decline and Fall*. Individual actors occupy the forefront of the stage to play their heroic, their comic, or their tragic roles; their vices, their crimes, and their virtues are exhibited, and they retire, leaving to others the continuation of the ever-changing and unending drama.

Gibbon assumes, as do most of his contemporaries, that human nature is essentially uniform, and that 'the different characters

[1] Edward Gibbon, *The History of the Decline and Fall of the Roman Empire*, J. B. Bury, ed. (7 vols., London, 1896–1900), ii. 529.

[2] (Paris, 1808), p. 121.

that mark the civilized nations of the globe may be ascribed to the use, and to the abuse, of reason'.[3] These assumptions make possible a variety of generalizations about man, and they underlie Gibbon's belief in the usefulness of history as a liberating study. After the manner of the ancients, he wrote history to instruct as well as to please. The instruction is of several kinds: philosophical, economic, political; but the ultimate value of history rests on moral grounds. Tacitus, who is praised whenever he is mentioned in *The Decline and Fall*, had written that history's highest function was 'to let no worthy action be uncommemorated, and to hold out the reprobation of posterity as a terror to evil words and deeds'.[4] Gibbon fully accepts this view. But in assuming the role of judge of the lives and actions of others, the historian takes on a very great, perhaps the greatest of responsibilities. A judge in a court of law has before him the legal codes of his country to guide him in his decisions. The historian has before him only the records of the past, his knowledge of human nature, and the values which he has been able to derive from the accumulated wisdom of mankind. Like the classical writers and the humanists of the Renaissance, who believed that a bad man could never write a great poem, Gibbon knew that a great work of history could result only from largeness of view, depth of understanding, and profound insight into human nature. In our own day Emery Neff was thinking of the same idea when he wrote, 'that historian is best who has the . . . most comprehensive mind and soul'.[5] The lifetime which Gibbon devoted to the study of classical and European civilization made him eminently qualified to create representations of human affairs and to judge them worthily.

The Roman custom at funerals and triumphs which corrected panegyric with satire resulted in a balanced judgement as the final comment on the life or on the actions of a particular man. It was a healthy custom, based on an honest recognition and frank acceptance of human fallibility. The same kind of balanced judgement is found in all the portraits of Gibbon. One of their most

[3] *The Decline and Fall*, iii. 71.

[4] 'Annals', 3.65, *Works*, A. J. Church and W. J. Brodribb, trans. (New York, 1942).

[5] *The Poetry of History* (New York, 1947), p. 199.

typical features is the delineation of virtues and vices with which each study concludes. In his portraits he achieved, wherever possible, the same clarity and perspicuity that he sought in all other matters in his history. Moreover, one is impressed by the variety of concrete detail with which the characters are drawn. Not only are the actions of important individuals presented vividly and dramatically, but also the facts of their birth and education, their tastes, judgements, and values, and the circumstances within which their lives are developed help to form the concrete pattern which embodies their spirit. With each of the major characters, such as Attila, Alaric, St. Bernard, and Clovis, Gibbon pauses to outline family background, early training, and often the character's economic circumstances before permitting him to enter the narrative. In the case of at least five characters—Alexander Severus, Julian, Sapor, Attila, and Theodoric—he devotes considerable space to a description of a typical day in the life of the man. The narrative of the actions, the struggles, the successes, and the failures of the individual is enlivened with anecdotes, often with brief speeches, sometimes with letters, and frequently with dramatically intense scenes. By the time the portrait is completed, the reader has gained a perfectly clear understanding of the nature of the man being described and of Gibbon's judgement of him. Moreover, the portrait has been animated with a touch of life: the great characters of *The Decline and Fall* have an existence apart from that of the author. In arranging the mass of concrete detail Gibbon is to a degree empathetic. The primary emphasis is on judgement and evaluation, but these matters need not and do not exclude the vital. If one revolves in his mind a few of the leading figures of the history—Julian, Athanasius, St. Ambrose, Mahomet, Justinian, Belisarius, Constantius, and Andronicus Comnenus—one will be impressed by the vitality and the extraordinary energy which they possess. Leslie Stephen's remark that 'A long series of historical figures passes before us in his stately pages, but they resemble the masks of a funeral procession',[6] may capture rather nicely the sense of pageantry; it suggests also the balance of praise and blame which Gibbon is so careful to achieve; but Gibbon's portraits are not funeral

[6] *History of English Thought in the Eighteenth Century* (2 vols., London, 1927), i. 447.

masks. The assessment of the significance of a life may have a funereal quality, but before we reach the summing up we are presented the living man. In an early work, the *Memoire sur la monarchie des Medes,* he commented upon one of the difficulties which beset the historical artist: 'Every man of genius who writes history infuses into it, perhaps unconsciously, the character of his own spirit. His characters, despite their extensive variety of passion and situation, seem to have only one manner of thinking and feeling, and that is the manner of the author.'[7] Such an awareness on the part of Gibbon could not help but guard against his own tendencies in this direction. Admittedly, Gibbon does use stock diction to describe and to interpret many of the attitudes as well as the actions of his characters. Their poses and gestures are too often the same; they blush or sigh or tremble; but what may seem to be a stylistic vice to a contemporary reader is more than offset by the rich variety of concrete detail which enables us to see clearly the individual's features. As a classical artist Gibbon is more concerned with the manifestation of the universal in the individual than with the idiosyncrasies of the particular man, but his interest in and allegiance to the concrete facts of history prevent him from allowing his characters to degenerate into types.

A useful example of Gibbon's manner of character drawing is seen in his portrait of the emperor Diocletian. He is neither one of the most important, nor one of the most perfectly drawn figures in *The Decline and Fall,* his role being overshadowed in the history by the great Constantine; but Gibbon's technique here is practised again and again, although it is always varied in the details of the pattern. We learn that Diocletian was born of slaves in the house of a Roman senator, that he early developed a consciousness of his own merit and took up the profession of arms as the quickest road to fortune. We learn, too, that he fought in the Persian war, where he distinguished himself. On the death of Numerian he was thought worthy of the purple. This rapid exposition culminates in the following quotation, which is introduced by Gibbon's noting that Diocletian has been unjustly accused of cowardice.

[7] *Miscellaneous Works of Edward Gibbon,* John, Lord Sheffield, ed. (5 vols., London, 1814), iii. 126. My translation.

The valour of Diocletian was never found inadequate to his duty, or to the occasion; but he appears not to have possessed the daring and generous spirit of a hero, who courts danger or fame, disdains artifice, and boldly challenges the allegiance of his equals. His abilities were useful rather than splendid; a vigorous mind, improved by the experience and study of mankind, dexterity and application in business; a judicious mixture of liberality and economy, of mildness and rigour; profound dissimulation under the disguise of military frankness; steadiness to pursue his ends; flexibility to vary his means; and above all the great art of submitting his own passions, as well as those of others, to the interest of his ambition, and of colouring his ambition with the most specious pretences of justice and public utility. Like Augustus, Diocletian may be considered as the founder of a new empire. Like the adopted son of Caesar, he was distinguished as a statesman rather than a warrior; nor did either of those princes employ force, whenever their purpose could be effected by policy.[8]

The passage is essential, in that it is a compressed, partly abstract representation of the spirit of the man as Gibbon conceives him. Coming at the beginning of the narrative of Diocletian's reign, it sets the keynote for the whole account. The specific actions of the emperor are illustrative of the ideas presented here. We see Diocletian as the founder of a new empire; we watch at a distance as he divides responsibility for the provinces, selects his associates, and directs his generals; and these matters are more intelligible because of the character which Gibbon has set before us at the opening of the chapter. The comparison with Augustus is sustained during the narrative and is another example of Gibbon's continuous commentary. The character, however, is not yet fully alive, still does not have what might be called an independent principle of motion. Not until we see how the emperor receives Galerius after he had lost his armies in the deserts of Mesopotamia does Diocletian the man begin to live for us:

Diocletian received him, not with the tenderness of a friend and colleague, but with the indignation of an offended sovereign. The haughtiest of men, clothed in his purple, but humbled by the sense of his fault and misfortune, was obliged to follow the emperor's chariot above a mile on foot, and to exhibit before the whole court the spectacle of his disgrace.[9]

[8] *The Decline and Fall*, i. 351.

[9] i. 370.

This brief incident with its inherent drama is followed by many larger and more important considerations: Diocletian's handling of the subsequent truce with Persia, the celebration of his triumph in Rome on the occasion of his twentieth year of rule, the policy of the new government which he established. In these matters Diocletian is partly hidden behind the mask of his position, yet small characterizing touches continuously remind the reader of the vital spirit within the breast of the emperor. We learn that on the news of Galerius's victory over the Persians, Diocletian 'condescended to advance towards the frontier, with a view of moderating, by his presence and councils, the pride of Galerius'.[10] We are told that after his Roman triumph Diocletian stayed a very short time in the eternal city.

> Disgusted with the licentious familiarity of the people, he quitted Rome with precipitation thirteen days before it was expected that he should have appeared in the senate, invested with the ensigns of the consular dignity.[11]

His thinking on the matter of the political value of imperial splendour and luxury, his political philosophy, and finally his decision to abdicate, continue Gibbon's characterization of the man. We get a brief glimpse of him after his dangerous illness in the year 304. He appears in public the following March, 'pale and emaciated'. We see him as he speaks at his abdication ceremony, and when Gibbon writes:

> As soon as he had divested himself of the purple, he withdrew from the gazing multitude, and, traversing the city in a covered chariot, proceeded, without delay, to the favourite retirement which he had chosen in his native country of Dalmatia.[12]

Diocletian's abdication is compared with those of other princes and an added anecdote vivifies the reader's understanding of the man. When he was solicited by Maximian to resume the reins of government:

> He rejected the temptation with a smile of pity, calmly observing that, if he could show Maximian the cabbages which he had planted

[10] i. 372. [11] i. 379. [12] i. 387.

with his own hands at Salona, he should no longer be urged to relinquish the enjoyment of happiness for the pursuit of power.[13]

The reader is then presented with some of the conversation of the emperor which has been preserved by contemporary writers. The topic is the art of ruling. Hard upon this detail follows a reference to the horrible persecution of Diocletian's wife and daughter by Licinius and Constantine, two men who had benefited greatly by the favour and by the power of the aged emperor. Gibbon concludes his portrait with the statement that Diocletian may have committed suicide to escape from the persecution of these same tyrants.

Diocletian returns to Gibbon's narrative in two other places. The first occasion is in a chapter concerned with the attitude of the Roman government towards the Christians from the reign of Nero to that of Constantine; the second takes up the political system of Diocletian and Constantine. But added information simply amplifies our understanding of the man. What we have seen is a careful portrait, presented at first in a description of the major features of his character, then illustrated by his actions as a man. The distant view is combined with the close; each can be said to complement the other. The combination of concrete detail with general assertion fulfils Gibbon's double purpose of representing a living character on the one hand and determining the significance and relative value of his actions on the other. The portrait is organized deductively, with the essential qualities of the character delineated first, and then illustrated by the narrative, the anecdote, and the final evaluation. The sustained comparison with Augustus is a focusing device which assists the reader in making a relative judgement. One other item in the portrait should be mentioned: Gibbon's description of Diocletian's palace which was constructed for his use in retirement. It has the value of illustrating the taste and interest of the emperor as well as the state of the arts in his age. Because of it we are better able to understand the man who chose cabbages instead of power as a preoccupation of his declining years.

An element in Gibbon's characterizations much more important than the accumulation of significant and revealing detail

[13] i. 388.

springs from the complex matter of the relation of the individual to his times. The tangled problem of distinguishing the proper share of responsibility for great events between the temper of the times and the genius of the individual is one to which Gibbon seems to have given considerable thought. D. M. Low and others have concluded that Gibbon's view of history was essentially dramatic, that the most important causes for events were to be found in the personalities and activities of the various leaders of the times. Such well-known passages as the following, when considered by themselves, seem to lend support to this thesis:

In the establishment and restoration of the Turkish empire, the first merit must doubtless be assigned to the personal qualities of the sultans; since in human life, the most important scenes will depend on the character of a single actor.[14]

This narrative of obscure and remote events is not foreign to the decline and fall of the Roman empire. If a Christian power had been maintained in Arabia, Mahomet must have been crushed in his cradle, and Abyssinia would have prevented a revolution which has changed the civil and religious state of the world.[15]

[Bajazet's] progress was checked, not by the miraculous interposition of the apostle, not by a crusade of the Christian powers, but by a long and painful fit of the gout. The disorders of the moral, are sometimes corrected by those of the physical, world; and an acrimonious humour falling on a single fibre of one man may prevent or suspend the misery of nations.[16]

It is true also that Gibbon follows his classical models in presenting speeches of various leaders, in dramatizing different scenes, and in discovering the means by which the passions of the multitude are combined and guided for the service of the leader. Under the conditions of tyranny, which are prevalent throughout most of *The Decline and Fall*, the personality, health, mental equipment, cultural background, and education of the tyrant naturally assume an importance much greater than they otherwise would, for as Louis XIV said, 'L'état, c'est moi!' But those who emphasize the dramatics of Gibbon's history forget that he was a student of Montesquieu, and that he wrote as a philosophic historian. He is concerned with the social consequences of luxury and pros-

[14] vii. 78. [15] iv. 387. [16] vii. 35.

perity, of military despotism and of the abuses of law and freedom at the same time that he is aware of the importance of the great man in specific historical events. In turning to a discussion of the new government formed by Diocletian and Constantine, he writes: 'This variety of objects will suspend, for some time, the course of the narrative; but the interruption will be censured only by those readers who are insensible to the importance of laws and manners, while they peruse, with eager curiosity, the transient intrigues of a court, or the accidental event of a battle.'[17] Furthermore, this study will 'tend to illustrate the secret and internal causes of [the empire's] rapid decay'.[18] Gibbon does not, like his successor Carlyle, subscribe to the great-man theory of history. The characteristics of nations and empires concern him as often as those of individuals. He speaks of the 'law of oriental dynasties'; he has a long section on the manners of pastoral nations; one entire chapter is devoted to a study of Roman jurisprudence, and at the very centre of *The Decline and Fall* is the law, which, according to Gibbon's understanding, reason has given to nature and nations. A great man can change the course of history but only by coming to grips with those impersonal forces operative in his times. Both the man and the temper of the age are taken into account in Gibbon's representation of any specific event. His interest as well as the nature of the material leads him to shift the emphasis from one to the other. In the portrait of Diocletian, for example, the emperor is primarily responsible for the specific forms which his new government took:

> Ostentation was the first principle of the new system instituted by Diocletian. The second was division. He divided the empire, the provinces, and every branch of the civil as well as military administration. He multiplied the wheels of the machine of government, and rendered its operations less rapid but more secure. Whatever advantages, and whatever defects, might attend these innovations, they must be ascribed in a very great degree to the first inventor. . . .[19]

Yet in the background is the sickness of the Roman world, a sickness which almost destroyed the empire prior to the reigns of the four princes of Illyricum. The transformation of the Roman government from the principate founded by Augustus into the

[17] ii. 158–9. [18] ii. 158. [19] i. 383.

absolute monarchy of Diocletian and his successor Constantine is an effort to resuscitate a dying culture. In Gibbon's portrait of Diocletian the larger forces of history supply a challenging context within which the great man is called upon to exercise his talents and his power. The times present him his opportunity; the way he uses the opportunity provides Gibbon with his richest means of characterization. In a passage near the end of the work we find him preoccupied with the same kind of relationship:

> It is an obvious truth that the times must be suited to extraordinary characters, and that the genius of Cromwell or Retz might now expire in obscurity. The political enthusiasm of Rienzi had exalted him to a throne; the same enthusiasm, in the next century, conducted his imitator to the gallows.[20]

Alexander Severus, for all his virtue, cannot arrest the corruption and the decay of discipline spreading over the Roman world. Julian is ineffectual in suppressing the growing power of the Christians. The strategies of Constantius and Julian are incapable of silencing the archbishop Athanasius. Alaric and Attila ride on a wave which is not altogether of their own making. Most of the merit of Claudius, Aurelian, Probus, and Diocletian lies in their restoring the Roman empire at a moment when its extinction is almost assured. Justinian and his generals Belisarius and Narses and even the Emperor Heraclius halt for a time the progress of decay. The response of the individual to the larger historical forces of his day is the source of the dramatic intensity of *The Decline and Fall*; it also provides our best understanding of the characters.

As an illustration we may consider Gibbon's treatment of the great Athanasius. When Gibbon was well along towards the completion of his history he recorded in a footnote that 'the portrait of Athanasius is one of the passages of my history . . . with which I am the least dissatisfied'.[21] Some observations on the manner in which this character is presented should, therefore, be of special interest.

The context in which we meet Athanasius is important. His life spanned the reigns of Constantius, Julian, and Jovian, and his sole preoccupation was the Arian controversy. When Gibbon

[20] vii. 293. [21] vi. 204, n. 101.

approaches his life, he pauses for a 'philosophic' observation. In addition to its other purposes in the history, the portrait is going to tell us something unusual about human nature.

> We have seldom an opportunity of observing, either in active or speculative life, what effect may be produced, or what obstacles may be surmounted, by the force of a single mind, when it is inflexibly applied to the pursuit of a single object. The immortal name of Athanasius will never be separated from the Catholic doctrine of the Trinity, to whose defence he consecrated every moment and every faculty of his being.[22]

The impact which the actions of this man make on the Church, on the Roman state, and on contemporaries will be Gibbon's special concern. The qualifications and talents of Athanasius for his self-appointed mission are examined next, and we find that he has a sinewy intellect and an extensive knowledge of human nature.

> He preserved a distinct and unbroken view of a scene which was incessantly shifting; and never failed to improve those decisive moments which are irrecoverably past before they are perceived by a common eye. The archbishop of Alexandria was capable of distinguishing how far he might boldly command, and where he must dexterously insinuate; how long he might contend with power, and when he must withdraw from persecution; and, while he directed the thunders of the church against heresy and rebellion, he could assume, in the bosom of his own party, the flexible and indulgent temper of a prudent leader.[23]

Indeed, Gibbon asserts that his superiority of character and abilities qualified him far better than the degenerate sons of Constantine to govern an empire. The comparison with the ruling emperors is significant because the drama of Athanasius's life arises altogether from his resistance to established power and from his triumph over authority.

In the larger structure of the work the portrait of Athanasius occurs at an historically significant moment. It is a time when the reader begins to witness a shift of power from the tyrants of the state to the princes of the Church. Constantine had made Christianity the official religion of the empire; but the church leaders

[22] ii. 361–2. [23] ii. 363.

had not yet won for themselves the power by which they could, as Gibbon puts it, trample on the necks of kings. Athanasius is a leader in this struggle, and as such he represents a new kind of hero: the militant church leader. He was the first of the Christians to humble the emperor of the Romans.

> In the height of his prosperity, . . . [Constantius], who had chastised the rashness of Gallus, and suppressed the revolt of Sylvanus, who had taken the diadem from the head of Vetranio, and vanquished in the field the legions of Magnentius, received from an invisible hand a wound which he could neither heal nor revenge; and the son of Constantine was the first of the Christian princes who experienced the strength of those principles which, in the cause of religion, could resist the most violent exertions of civil power.[24]

The career of Athanasius brings him into direct conflict with another kind of hero. The life and reign of Julian the Apostate contain many characteristics of ancient Roman greatness. Just as Julian is representative of a whole culture which is seen on the ebb, so Athanasius embodies within his life and actions the rising culture of institutionalized Christianity. Since Gibbon's subject is the fall of Rome, Julian's rise to fame, his efforts to restore paganism, and his disastrous Persian expedition comprise the major theme in the three chapters given to his reign. The activities of Athanasius, which are treated as a growing and increasingly serious irritation, are a minor theme. The destinies of both men are brought into direct conflict in the middle chapter, which is concerned with Julian's religion. 'Julian, who despised the Christians, honoured Athanasius with his sincere and peculiar hatred', Gibbon writes, and in a single sentence he embraces the antagonism of the two men and the ultimate achievements of their lives.

> The archbishop prudently retired to the monasteries of the Desert: eluded, with his usual dexterity, the snares of the enemy; and lived to triumph over the ashes of a prince who, in words of formidable import, had declared his wish that the whole venom of the Galilaean school were contained in the single person of Athanasius.[25]

The conflict between Athanasius and Julian is a contest for control of the fate of mankind. The emperor of the Romans in the pursuit

[24] ii. 380–1.

[25] ii. 475–6.

of fame wished to conquer and subdue the nations of the earth. His ruling passion was the love of glory. The aim of Athanasius was not very different: it was the spiritual conquest of the earth.

> Five times was Athanasius expelled from his throne; twenty years he passed as an exile or a fugitive; and almost every province of the Roman empire was successively witness to his merit, and his sufferings in the cause of the Homoousion, which he considered as the sole pleasure and business, as the duty, and as the glory, of his life.[26]

Indeed, when reviewing Gibbon's dramatization of this struggle one is impressed as much by the similarity of the contending parties as by their differences. He suggests their similarity with the remark that 'the Christians had forgotten the spirit of the Gospel; and the Pagans had imbibed the spirit of the church'.[27] Both leaders are capable of tyranny, and the last of the emperors who tried to destroy Christianity meets an enemy worthy of his own powers.

> The state of the Christian world was present to his [i.e. Athanasius] active and capacious mind; and the age, the merit, the reputation of Athanasius enabled him to assume, in a moment of danger, the office of Ecclesiastical Dictator.[28]

The temper of the times was on the side of Athanasius, and with the premature death of Julian, Gibbon asserts:

> Christianity obtained an easy and lasting victory; and, as soon as the smile of royal patronage was withdrawn, the genius of paganism, which had been fondly raised and cherished by the arts of Julian, sunk irrecoverably in the dust.[29]

There is good reason to believe that when Gibbon contemplated executing his history only as far as the extinction of the empire of the West, he planned the reign of Julian the Apostate as the climax of the work. Certainly the supposition is supported by the manner in which he contrasts Julian and Athanasius. Readers of *Paradise Lost* will remember Milton's careful arrangement of his material so that a strong contrast between Christ and Satan underscores the meaning of the epic. In a similar fashion, and to the extent which the facts of history permit, Gibbon achieves a

[26] ii. 362. [27] iii. 1. [28] ii. 473. [29] iii. 3.

contrast between the pagan hero and the new hero of the Christian Church. The contrast emerges at a critical point of the history. Although I have mentioned *Paradise Lost* only for purposes of illustration, support for my comparison of the art of Gibbon with that of Milton is derived from the fact that at least twice in his account of Julian the Apostate Gibbon uses the same language which Milton had used for Satan. But unlike Milton, who saw perfection, human and divine, in Christ, Gibbon chooses neither the Roman hero nor Athanasius to represent his ideal. Julian, for all his strength of mind and nobility of character, is a superstitious idolator; and his love of military glory brings about a major defeat for the legions along with his own destruction. Athanasius, whatever may be his talents, is both fanatical and proud; his life was dedicated to establishing as inflexible dogma an impenetrable mystery.

My discussion so far has been concerned with the larger historical issues which are represented in the lives and actions of two men. It is a great mistake, however, to take Gibbon's portraits as mere symbols, for Athanasius, as well as Julian, is a sharply individualized character. The significant events of his life are presented with considerable immediacy. His actions may illustrate, modify, or simply move with, the great, glacier-like forces of history, but primary attention is given to the man. We see Athanasius in exile, at the synod, in the court, and at such exciting moments as the following:

On the memorable night when the church of St. Theonas was invested by the troops of Syrianus, the archbishop, seated on his throne, expected, with calm and intrepid dignity, the approach of death. While the public devotion was interrupted by shouts of rage and cries of terror, he animated his trembling congregation to express their religious confidence, by chanting one of the psalms of David, which celebrates the triumph of the God of Israel over the haughty and impious tyrant of Egypt. The doors were at length burst open; a cloud of arrows was discharged among the people; the soldiers, with drawn swords, rushed forwards into the sanctuary; and the dreadful gleam of their armour was reflected by the holy luminaries which burnt round the altar. Athanasius still rejected the pious importunity of the Monks and Presbyters, who were attached to his person; and nobly refused to desert his episcopal station, till he had dismissed in safety the last of the congregation. The darkness and tumult of the night favoured the retreat of the archbishop; and, though he was oppressed by the waves of an agitated multitude, though he was thrown to the ground, and left without sense or motion, he still recovered his undaunted courage, and eluded the eager search of the soldiers, who were instructed by their Arian guides that the head of Athanasius would be the most acceptable present to the emperor.[30]

With such passages Gibbon conducts the narrative of the extraordinary life of this fascinating person; but the drama is greatly intensified by the significant relation of these specific events to the dominant historical forces of the age in which they occur. The conjunction of historically fertile times and men of genius tends to make some of the characters in Gibbon larger than life. Both Julian and Athanasius are giants in the earth.

The relationship of the individual to his times is also the source of a continuing but flexible standard of judgement. Gibbon expands this idea in his comments on the achievements of Belisarius.

Our estimate of personal merit is relative to the common faculties of mankind. The aspiring efforts of genius or virtue, either in active or speculative life, are measured not so much by their real elevation as by the height to which they ascend above the level of their age or country; and the same stature, which in a people of giants would pass unnoticed, must appear conspicuous in a race of pygmies. Leonidas and his three hundred companions devoted their lives at Thermopylae; but the education of the infant, the boy, and the man, had prepared, and almost ensured, this memorable sacrifice; and each Spartan would approve, rather than admire an act of duty of which himself and eight thousand of his fellow-citizens were equally capable.[31]

If one takes this approach, the character of Belisarius must be rated very high indeed, Gibbon continues, so high that it 'may be deservedly placed above the heroes of the ancient republics'.

His imperfections flowed from the contagion of the times; his virtues were his own, the free gift of nature or reflection; he raised himself without a master or a rival; and so inadequate were the arms committed to his hand that his sole advantage was derived from the pride and presumption of his adversaries.[32]

[30] ii. 377–8. [31] iv. 340. [32] iv. 340–1.

In the same view, the phenomenal rise and meteor-like splendour of Rienzi, who for a very brief interval lighted the dark night of Roman slavery, takes on less value. He is presented as a man cast by history into a role of fame, and he appears all the weaker by his inability to play the role as the times demanded. The acceptance of public responsibility on the part of the senator Boethius is more impressive because of the prevailing barbarism of his age, and Gibbon calls him 'the last of the Romans whom Cato or Tully could have acknowledged for their countryman'.[33] The poet Claudian acquires a lustre from the fact that he, alone, in dark and degenerate times kept alive the spirit of poetry. And the heroism of the last of the Byzantine emperors, Constantine Palaeologus, who died defending Constantinople, blazes forth from the crowd of his pusillanimous subjects.

The relation of the individual to his age is only one standard of judgement, and it is a shifting one. Gibbon also measures the accomplishments and merit of individuals against an abstract standard which represents his idea of the perfection of human nature. The paragraph in which this ideal is explicitly described occurs, significantly, in his discussion of the dissemination of Christianity and has been quoted in my second chapter. From various scattered comments by which he completes the picture, we can conclude that the true hero of Gibbon's thinking is a man occupied with affairs of this world and with his responsibilities to his fellow creatures. He seeks private and public happiness and is willing to exert himself for the achievement of both. His education is liberal, in the classical sense of that term. He is a man prepared, as were the Romans of the great days of the republic, to fulfil all the offices of private and public life. He is a man in whom the raw material of human nature has been refined and developed according to the precepts of the best pagan thinkers. His understanding has been enlarged by a study of letters; his virtue is found in the golden mean of the Greeks; and in his life he approaches the Aristotelian concept of the magnanimous man. His religion consists of humility before the author of all things, whom he cannot presume to understand. His mind is free from the tyranny of superstition, passion, and the appetites, and he is obedient to the dictates of right reason. He is a man of these

[33] iv. 197–8.

virtues, whatever role he must play, be it that of statesman, general, orator, or poet. In his general comments Gibbon continually brings his reader back to his clearly defined standard. In speaking of barbarians elevated by Constantine to positions of authority as a reward for their services, he writes:

> But as these hardy veterans, who had been educated in the ignorance or contempt of the laws, were incapable of exercising any civil offices, the powers of the human mind were contracted by the irreconcileable separation of talents as well as of professions. The accomplished citizens of the Greek and Roman republics, whose characters could adapt themselves to the bar, the senate, the camp, or the schools, had learned to write, to speak, and to act, with the same spirit, and with equal abilities.[34]

The closest representations of this ideal are characters who do not, properly speaking, enter *The Decline and Fall* except in so far as they provide points of reference. Like Julian in his *Caesars*, Gibbon would give the crown for perfection of human nature to Marcus Antoninus; he would extend it also to Cicero, Homer, and Tacitus, to mention only a few. In his 'Vindication' he singles out as the wisest and most virtuous of the pagans Trajan and the Antonines, Homer and Euripides, Plato and Aristotle.[35] Like Julian, Gibbon would rule out certain other close contenders for the crown on the grounds of ambition for military fame. We find him paraphrasing Milton in his description of John the Handsome: 'The only defect of this accomplished character was the frailty of noble minds, the love of arms and military glory.'[36] Specific individuals partake of some of the virtues listed in my summary, but in most of the characters who pass through Gibbon's pages these qualities are more conspicuous by their absence. Wherever possible he makes the effort to balance a character's virtues with his vices, his strengths with his weaknesses, his magnanimous actions with his petty concerns. Although perfection in human nature is viewed as attainable, and, indeed, the goal towards which man should strive if he is to fulfil his destiny, there is nothing sanguine in Gibbon's thinking on the matter of how far mankind is from achieving it. On the contrary, the

[34] ii. 181–2.
[35] *Miscellaneous Works*, iv. 545.
[36] v. 229.

readers of *The Decline and Fall* are soberly impressed by the astonishing aberrations from Gibbon's ideal.

The manner in which the standard is applied varies considerably in *The Decline and Fall.* Sometimes, as in the following example, Gibbon's reference to the ideal is specific. He is speaking about Leo VI, emperor of Constantinople:

> . . . the union of the prince and the sage, of the active and speculative virtues, would indeed constitute the perfection of human nature. But the claims of Leo are far short of this ideal excellence. Did he reduce his passions and appetites under the dominion of reason? . . . Did he subdue his prejudices, and those of his subjects? His mind was tinged with the most puerile superstition. . . .[37]

Or Gibbon will introduce other concepts of the hero, other ways of conceiving the perfection of human nature.

> The name of Alp Arslan, the valiant lion, is expressive of the popular idea of the perfection of man; and the successor of Togrul displayed the fierceness and generosity of the royal animal.[38]

About Richard I of England, Gibbon comments:

> . . . if heroism be confined to brutal and ferocious valour, Richard Plantagenet will stand high among the heroes of the age.[39]

A different kind of thinking on perfection in human life, involving in these examples no particular reference to individuals but revealing a standard which is later applied to specific characters, is found in Gibbon's comments on pastoral life and on contemporary ideas of the noble savage. He has few illusions, and the supposed idyllic life of shepherds does not deceive him.

> . . . the sober historian is forcibly awakened from a pleasing vision; and is compelled, with some reluctance, to confess that the pastoral manners which have been adorned with the fairest attributes of peace and innocence are much better adapted to the fierce and cruel habits of a military life.[40]

And perhaps he is thinking specifically of Rousseau when he describes the inhumanity of the Thuringians:

37 v. 206–7.

38 vi. 236.

39 vi. 350.

40 iii. 71–72.

> They massacred their hostages, as well as their captives: two hundred young maidens were tortured with exquisite and unrelenting rage; their bodies were torn asunder by wild horses, or their bones were crushed under the weight of rolling waggons; and their unburied limbs were abandoned on the public roads, as a prey to dogs and vultures. Such were those savage ancestors, whose imaginary virtues have sometimes excited the praise and envy of civilized ages.[41]

If it is man's destiny to cultivate and develop his reason, his virtues, and the arts of civilization, then the savage is an ignoble and imperfect representative of his species. In speaking of the ancient Germans, Gibbon uses typical irony: 'They passed their lives in a state of ignorance and poverty, which it has pleased some declaimers to dignify with the appellation of virtuous simplicity.'[42] The application of these ideas to specific individuals offers him one more means by which he can delineate character with precision.

Perhaps the most sustained contrast between different concepts of human perfection is seen in Gibbon's treatment of the Christians. In their thinking about the nature of man and in their theological systems, in their ideas of virtue and in their heroes, they differ radically from Gibbon. His remarks on the theology of Saint Augustine are typical:

> . . . he boldly sounded the dark abyss of grace, predestination, freewill, and original sin; and the rigid system of Christianity, which he framed or restored, has been entertained, with public applause and secret reluctance, by the Latin church.[43]

Far from accepting the idea of original sin, Gibbon founded his idea of the true nature of man on Plato's metaphor of the charioteer driving one good and one bad horse, the good creature continually aspiring to the true and the beautiful, the bad horse, unruly and violent, trying to drag down to his own bestial level the human soul. Even in the grossest barbarism elements of the good are apparent, just as in the most highly cultivated societies the struggle for control of the darker side of human nature must be continued. Nor does Gibbon accept Christian ideas of hell, purgatory, and paradise. He even goes so far as to suggest that the idea of hell and eternal damnation is an outrage to human nature:

[41] iii. 467. [42] i. 218. [43] iii. 407.

The bishops of Tours and Milan pronounced, without hesitation, the eternal damnation of heretics; but they were surprised, and shocked, by the bloody image of their temporal death, *and the honest feelings of nature resisted* the artificial prejudices of theology.[44]

Not only important parts of Christian dogma, but also some Christian institutions are, in Gibbon's view, repulsive and insulting to the dignity of man. Of the Inquisition, for example, he writes, it was 'an office more adapted to confirm, than to refute, the belief of an evil principle'.[45] There is also a sharp dichotomy between Gibbon's idea of virtue and what he continually refers to as the meek and humble virtues of the followers of Christ. The dogma of Christianity and the heroes of the new religion are often for him the subjects of satire. I shall take up the whole question of Gibbon's irony and his use of satire in the next chapter, but I should like to conclude these observations on the manner in which Gibbon contrasts different concepts of the ideal in human nature by noting some of his comments on the saints, the heroes of Christianity.

On saints in general we find a typical remark: 'The merits and miracles of the whole calendar are of less account in the eyes of a sage than the toil of a single husbandman, who multiplies the gifts of the Creator and supplies the food of his brethren.'[46] Indeed, there is in almost all of Gibbon's references to saints a sharply drawn antithesis between the merit of sainthood and humanity. Speaking of the reflections of the Archbishop Gregory on the manner of his appointment to the throne, Gibbon says: 'But the saint (who had not subdued the imperfections of human virtue) was deeply affected by the mortifying consideration that his entrance into the fold was that of a wolf, rather than of a shepherd. . . .'[47] The antithesis is seen in another remark: 'The title of Saint has been added to his name; but the tenderness of his heart and the elegance of his genius reflect a more pleasing lustre on the memory of Gregory Nazianzen.'[48] And as a final illustration we should note what Gibbon says of Saint Bernard: 'he seems to have preserved as much reason and humanity as may be reconciled with the character of a saint'.[49]

The power of Gibbon's characterizations is the result of extra-

[44] iii. 155. Italics mine. [45] vi. 125. [46] vi. 64–65.
[47] iii. 147. [48] iii. 151. [49] vi. 333.

ordinary precision in the delineation of detail, in the measurement and evaluation of specific qualities, both as they relate to the times in which the character moves in history, and as they relate to the abstract and absolute standard of goodness which he has been careful to describe. The drama of an individual's life is greatly intensified by Gibbon's stress of its immediate significance to the period in history in which the character lives. The philosophic historian would have his readers learn from the experiences of the actors in his history lessons for the guidance and conduct of their own lives. Gibbon hoped that the readers of *The Decline and Fall* would find in his volumes the same usefulness which the Emperor Theodosius found in his reading: 'The annals of Rome, in the long period of eleven hundred years, presented him with a various and splendid picture of human life; and it has been particularly observed that, whenever he perused the cruel acts of Cinna, of Marius, or of Sylla, he warmly expressed his generous detestation of those enemies of humanity and freedom. His disinterested opinion of past events was usefully applied as a rule of his own actions. . . .'[50]

[50] iii. 167.

VI · SATIRE

> [Gibbon] . . ., deep and slow, exhausting thought,
> And hiving wisdom with each studious year,
> In meditation dwelt, with learning wrought,
> And shaped his weapon with an edge severe,
> Sapping a solemn creed with solemn sneer;
> The lord of irony,—
>
> *Childe Harold's Pilgrimage,* III. cvii

IT is not surprising that *The Decline and Fall* contains a great variety of satire. The writer who selected Juvenal as his close companion and who once characterized history as a record of the crimes and follies of mankind would surely in a description of fourteen centuries of human history be exercised in the various techniques of social and moral criticism. These centuries saw the tremendous fall from greatness of the empire of Rome; they were centuries which more often than not witnessed the abuse rather than the cultivation of human reason and virtue. The satirist is engaged in measuring aberrations from the ideal, and the departure from the ideals of Greece and Rome was to Gibbon a major aberration. Furthermore, hypocrisy, vice, pretension, and pedantry are constants in human nature: second-century Rome or eighteenth-century England alike turn up many examples. Moreover, the particular evils of any specific age are also the proper concern of the historian.

The uses of satire in a work that presumes to be a truthful representation of the past can be more sympathetically understood if one remembers that to Gibbon and his age history was moral in its function. One should note also that Gibbon was not tyrannized by the relativism in values and morality which so vitiates contemporary satire. Appealing to a commonly shared and rationally approved body of ideals, the historian was able to use satire to lash folly, vice, and intolerance without ever descending from the disinterested pursuit of truth. It protects him from the indignities of hostile vituperation, and, as an instrument of judgement, it is capable of enforcing a lesson gracefully and skilfully. It is a source of entertainment, and it lightens a narrative which would otherwise sink under the burden of enormous calamities. As the orator delivering a long memorial address, Gibbon is in complete control of his material and of his audience. The means by which he uses his position for the purposes of satire are the concern of the present chapter.

Of the various forms of satire found in *The Decline and Fall*, irony is perhaps the most common. Fowler, in his *Handbook of English Usage*, has distinguished three different species of irony in literature. The first is the well-known Socratic type, in which the speaker, professing his own ignorance, leads on those he questions or those with whom he converses to an unmasking of their own ignorance. The second is the familiar dramatic irony which consists of a play between two audiences: the one initiated and aware of matters hidden from the other. The third type is called cosmic irony and results from a conflict of human understanding with the events of life and nature. The mind is always seeking coherence and meaning in the apparent chaos of human affairs; irony results from the fact that the events of life often destroy the supposed pattern and suggest in its place another, undreamt-of meaning. This last kind is sometimes called the irony of fate. One of Gibbon's peculiar literary merits is that all three kinds of irony are employed extensively in *The Decline and Fall*. In fact, much of his work deserves to stand beside the irony of Swift as the best representation of this genre in English.

In the larger view, *The Decline and Fall* can be seen as constructed on the double base of cosmic and dramatic irony. Dramatic irony arises from the fact that the actors are unaware of the full view of their conduct which the detachment of the historian permits to himself and his readers. Cosmic irony results from the apparent contradiction of human nature that a creature such as man, endowed with the power of reason, should demonstrate in so many ways his incapacity or his unwillingness to use it as his guide. Seen in this light, the cosmic irony of *The Decline and Fall* penetrates to the very core of human life and accounts for the tone of genuine tragedy which lies at the centre of the whole work. Many readers have noticed the optimism of Gibbon's commentaries on his own age and on the real progress in human affairs which he thought he was able to record. But not enough attention has been paid to his deep awareness of the terrifying cost in human life and values which has purchased this progress. Looking down from the summit of a philosophic age, Gibbon may very well disdain the fleeting phantoms who lived and died in ignorant and ignoble turmoil; but we should never forget that the same Gibbon describes Tamburlaine's pyramids of human heads, the indiscriminate slaughter of hundreds of thousands of civilians, and the sacks of human ears collected by the Moguls. He also wrote: 'if we are more deeply affected by the ruin of a palace than by the conflagration of a cottage, our humanity must have formed a very erroneous estimate of the miseries of human life'.[1] The cosmic irony of *The Decline and Fall* does not exclude pity and terror. Man has more to fear from the fierce operation of his own passions, Gibbon writes, than from all the convulsions of nature, and the pages of *The Decline and Fall* provide ample testimony to the truth of this statement. Because Gibbon and his age had such a lofty view of what man might be, their examination of the record of the past is charged with a sense of the terrible. Basil Willey was thinking of the same idea when he wrote: 'If you worship "Nature and Reason" you will be the more afflicted by human unreason; and perhaps only the effort to see man as the world's glory will reveal how far he is really its jest and riddle.'[2]

Irony as an ally of tragedy is further seen in the first three chapters of *The Decline and Fall,* where the summit of prosperity is discovered to contain within it the seeds of its own decay. The contrast between apparent happiness and real evil permeates Gibbon's description of the Roman world. Ending on the edge of slavery and destruction, these chapters cut deeply into our notion of the greatness of human accomplishment. The melancholy theme is picked up in the last three chapters of the work where we witness the futile attempts of the now fully degenerate Romans to restore their liberty and to recapture their past glory. In the span of fourteen centuries we have witnessed the struggles and aspirations of mankind: thousands of figures, gods and heroes, tyrants and republicans, slaves and soldiers, have ended in a

[1] *The History of the Decline and Fall of the Roman Empire*, J. B. Bury, ed. (7 vols., London, 1896–1900), ii. 499.

[2] *The Eighteenth Century Background* (London, 1949), p. 100.

common grave. The reader who wishes to find in human life a lasting significance sees the tremendous drama of man's affairs finally overwhelmed by the iron sleep of death.

Gibbon's ironic techniques are seen more specifically in his treatment of Christianity. His case against the Church involves both the introduction of Christianity to the Roman world and the abuses of its doctrines. The irony in his discussion of the introduction of Christianity is based on his sceptical and rationalistic approach to divine revelation and on his temperamental incapacity to appreciate sympathetically the regenerative power of Christian love. The irony in his discussion of the abuses of Christianity results largely from his simply requiring that Christians live up to their professed ideals. His case against Christianity is quite clear. He believed that in aspiring to the happiness of a future life, the Christians created much real misery in this life:

> The clergy successfully preached the doctrines of patience and pusillanimity; the active virtues of society were discouraged; and the last remains of the military spirit were buried in the cloister. . . .[3]

Ignorant of their own nature, the leaders of the Church had the arrogance to define the nature of God and to explain the mysteries of heaven and hell. In the name of an unknown and unseen power, they perpetrated the most enormous civil crimes:

> It has been computed that one hundred thousand Roman subjects were extirpated in the Samaritan war, which converted the once fruitful province into a desolate and smoking wilderness. But in the creed of Justinian the guilt of murder could not be applied to the slaughter of unbelievers; and he piously laboured to establish with fire and sword the unity of the Christian faith.[4]

In hammering out the minute details of dogma the bishops created a chain with which to bind the human mind and inhibit it from its natural function of free speculation. Like one of Milton's fallen angels, Gibbon would choose

> Though full of pain, this intellectual being,
> Those thoughts that wander through eternity.

Moreover, he believed that in the service of God the Christians frequently forgot the service of man.

[3] *The Decline and Fall*, iv. 162–3. [4] v. 136.

> In the last and fatal siege [of Syracuse—A.D. 877], her citizens displayed some remnant of the spirit which had formerly resisted the powers of Athens and Carthage. They stood about twenty days against the battering-rams and *catapultae*, the mines and tortoises, of the besiegers; and the place might have been relieved, if the mariners of the Imperial fleet had not been detained at Constantinople in building a church to the Virgin Mary.[5]

The virtues of charity and love were forgotten. Instead of tolerance, Christianity too often produced intolerance; instead of forgiveness of enemies, hatred and ruthless persecution; instead of truth, pious deception and fraud.

There is nothing new in this indictment. Students of the Enlightenment will have no trouble in adding to it. 'Écrasez l'infâme', wrote Voltaire, and many of his contemporaries sought to do just that. But Gibbon calls Voltaire a bigot, and he wrote apropos of Helvétius and d'Holbach that he could not approve the intolerant zeal of the philosophers and the Encyclopedists. As an historian, Gibbon seeks to assess impartially and judiciously the significance of events in the past. Where he differs from most of his contemporaries is in the thoroughness of his scholarship and his genuine interest in discovering exactly how much can be ascertained by a secular inquiry into the field of theological history. His irony is not simply a negative, destructive weapon. He does not hide behind it, refusing to commit himself as to his own values and ideals. It does not provide a mode of escape for him by which he can avoid the responsibilities and fundamental problems of life. In the name of rationalism he uses irony to attack zeal, enthusiasm, fanaticism, and even faith, but he does so in an effort which is essentially constructive. He seeks to liberate the human mind from what he considers to be its strongest fetters. Many writers have noted that Gibbon is, as Byron put it, engaged in 'sapping a solemn creed with a solemn sneer', but insufficient attention has been paid to the fact that he does so in an effort to celebrate the values of intellectual and spiritual freedom.

When considered by itself, however, the famous, or perhaps I should say notorious, fifteenth chapter, which undertakes a study of the dissemination of Christianity, is a partial exception to these

[5] vi. 39

observations; for there is no question but that here Gibbon uses the role of a disinterested, detached historian as a shield behind which he can carry on a wholesale destructive operation. Boswell said about it that there should have been a warning, 'springs and traps set here', and his view was shared by many of his contemporaries. This chapter, and the one following it, which is a study of the conduct of the Romans towards the Christians from the time of Nero to the reign of Constantine, brought down the wrath of churchmen on the historian's head. Gibbon himself, who later referred to 'the indifferent religion' of his own day, was surprised by the outburst, and perhaps his surprise was not an affectation. In any event, it was not until his scholarship was attacked and his integrity arraigned that he was moved to reply to his outraged critics. His *Vindication* remains an example of deadly polemic in which he acquits himself once and for all from charges of factual inaccuracy. None the less, the inferences which must be drawn from the facts are thoroughly hostile to Christianity.

The irony used in the fifteenth chapter may be called, with some reservations, Socratic; and it is probably not an accident that Gibbon took the favourite instrument of the wisest pagan to implement his discussion of the fate and teachings of the first and best Christian. Behind the discussion can be seen the shadowy figures of Christ and Socrates, but Gibbon does not bring them directly into the study. Its subject rather is what men have done with the teachings of these great figures.

Like Socrates, Gibbon takes for himself a modest role in the discussion. The question is raised as to how Christianity obtained such a signal victory over the established religions of the earth. There is an obvious answer: it was the truth of the doctrine and the providence of its great author. Yet the historian cannot be fully satisfied with this answer for 'truth and reason seldom find so favourable reception in the world, and . . . Providence frequently condescends to use the passions of the human heart, and the general circumstances of mankind . . . to execute its purpose'.[6] It is because of these reasons that the historian 'may still be permitted, *though with becoming submission,* to ask not indeed what were the first, but what were the secondary causes of the rapid growth of the Christian church'.[7] With these words Gibbon

[6] ii. 2. [7] Ibid. Italics mine.

undertakes an investigation never before made from a purely secular point of view. No longer was church history the exclusive province of the theologians. For them was reserved the pleasant task of 'describing religion as she descended from heaven', but for the historian there rested the more melancholy duty of discovering 'the inevitable mixture of error and corruption which she contracted in a long residence upon earth . . .'.[8]

The key instruments of Gibbon's irony are thus created. The separation of history from theology is, from the Church's point of view, impossible, for history is simply the drama of God's providence. The study of the ways of God rests on faith. But the study of man and the secondary causes of the growth of his religion is justifiably the proper concern of a reasonable inquiry. Gibbon seems to be asking for only a little, and he asks for it disarmingly. On the side of reason is the great law of impartiality; on the side of faith, divine revelation. The irony in this chapter results from a sustained commentary of the secondary causes on the validity of the accepted doctrine of the first. Like Socrates, Gibbon seeks to discover only what may be ascertained, and the net result in this case is that so much error and weakness can be discovered by a study of secondary causes that knowledge of the primary cause is almost buried under high-piled doubts. Gibbon guards his flanks by facing in advance any threat which might seem to come from these directions. He openly states that

> The great law of impartiality too often obliges us to reveal the imperfections of the uninspired teachers and believers of the gospel; and, to a careless observer, *their* faults may seem to cast a shade on the faith which they professed. But the scandal of the pious Christian, and the fallacious triumph of the Infidel, should cease as soon as they recollect not only *by whom,* but likewise *to whom,* the Divine Revelation was given.[9]

With this remark Gibbon throws his opponents back to the tenets of their faith; it is not the duty of an historian to explain why God chose to reveal His will in the way He is supposed to have done. The theologians can do that and are put in a position where they must do that. But the historian can and should study 'the weak and degenerate race of beings' who were the recipients and

[8] ii. 2. [9] ii. 1–2.

custodians of the Divine Word. Despite protestations to the contrary, Gibbon inevitably proceeds from this position to what may be loosely called an *ad hominem* argument. By showing the errors, the illogicalities, and the weaknesses of men, he seeks to invalidate their interpretation of the ways of God. Nowhere in this chapter does he attack Christian dogma directly, but he has its strongest defenders display their arguments and their conduct. The result is that Christ and God are excluded from the discussion, but human conceptions of them, their nature and their teaching, are not. There is a strain running through the chapter which suggests Mark Antony's remarks about the honourable Brutus, and it is used in the same way. With numerous variations, it runs: 'It is incumbent upon us to adore the mysterious dispensations of Providence when we discover', &c. The ways of Providence defy rational inquiry.

A typical example of the ironist at work can be found in Gibbon's discussion of the Mosaic religion. I should like to dwell briefly on the key paragraph. In his enumeration of the five secondary causes of Christianity's triumph, the first was 'the inflexible, and . . . intolerant zeal of the Christians, derived, . . . from the Jewish religion'.[10] His thesis in this section is that Christianity offered itself to the world, 'armed with the strength of Mosaic law, and delivered from the weight of its fetters'. The Jews are described as the most intolerant of all the peoples of the ancient world. Even though numerically small, this people persisted through successive calamities in its unsocial religion and detestation of foreign nations. Then follows the first of many shrewd ironic thrusts. 'This inflexible perseverance, which appeared so odious, or so ridiculous, to the ancient world, assumes a more awful character, since Providence has deigned to reveal to us the mysterious history of the chosen people.' It is awful because of its astonishing illogicality.

But the devout, and even scrupulous, attachment to the Mosaic religion, so conspicuous among the Jews who lived under the second temple, becomes still more surprising, if it is compared with the stubborn incredulity of their forefathers. When the law was given in thunder from Mount Sinai; when the tides of the ocean and the course of the planets were suspended for the convenience of the Israelites;

[10] ii. 2.

and when temporal rewards and punishments were the immediate consequences of their piety or disobedience; they perpetually relapsed into rebellion against the visible majesty of their Divine King, placed the idols of the nations in the sanctuary of Jehovah, and imitated every fantastic ceremony that was practised in the tents of the Arabs or in the cities of Phoenicia.[11]

The continual backsliding of the Israelites under Moses, the judges, and the kings, is used to suggest that the preternatural events of the Old Testament are mere fables. But since they are accepted as truthful revelations of the ways of Providence, we can only adore the mystery. The incredulity of the ancient Hebrews is as hard to explain as the credulity of the Jews under the second temple. Gibbon has yet to climax his paragraph. The sword has been thrust in, and now he can twist it:

> The contemporaries of Moses and Joshua had beheld, with careless indifference, the most amazing miracles. Under the pressure of every calamity, the belief of those miracles has preserved the Jews of a later period from the universal contagion of idolatry; and, *in contradiction to every known principle of the human mind,* that singular people seems to have yielded a stronger and more ready assent to the traditions of their remote ancestors than to the evidence of their own senses.[12]

I have quoted much of this long paragraph because it illustrates a central technique of Gibbon's irony. The illogicalities, the inconsistencies of religious dogma are used to undermine the base on which it rests. Like Socrates, Gibbon lets dogma tell its own story, but in such a way as to illustrate whatever inherent logical fallacies and weaknesses it might have. Also, like Socrates, he is content to seem merely to raise questions or, as in the following example, to underscore apparent absurdities when he finds them. Of the conversion of the Goths, who, unfortunately, imbibed the Arian heresy along with the truth of the Gospel, he writes: 'The heroes of the North, who had submitted, with some reluctance, to believe that all their ancestors were in hell, were astonished and exasperated to learn that they themselves had only changed the mode of their eternal condemnation.'[13]

The pose of the ironist is carefully established and always main-

[11] ii. 4. [12] Ibid. Italics mine. [13] iv. 81.

tained. It is that of a calm, modest, and reasonable man, seeking in so far as possible to ascertain the facts. He often dramatizes the virtue of his own position by contrasting it with the anger, the arrogance, and the irrationality of the dogmatists. For example, the humanity and tolerance of Gibbon shine against the background of bitter invective in the following quotation which he draws from the works of Tertullian: '"How shall I admire, how laugh, how rejoice, how exult,"' writes Tertullian, '"when I behold so many proud monarchs, and fancied gods, groaning in the lowest abyss of darkness; so many magistrates, who persecuted the name of the Lord, liquifying in fiercer fires than they ever kindled against the Christians; so many sage philosophers blushing in red hot flames, with their deluded scholars; so many celebrated poets trembling before the tribunal, not of Minos, but of Christ; so many tragedians, more tuneful in the expression of their own sufferings; so many dancers . . .".'[14] Gibbon stops here with the remark that the humanity of the reader will permit him to draw a veil over the rest of this infernal description. One should not fail to observe that the ironist resolves by contrasts such as this the basic problem of satire and wins the approbation of his audience for his own position while directing their hostility towards that of his enemies. If we are to choose between Gibbon and Tertullian, as long as humanity and tolerance affect our choice there can be little hesitation. Gibbon draws back from the noisy violence of this horrid display with the remark: 'Doubtless there were many among the primitive Christians of a temper more suitable to the meekness and charity of their profession.'

The fifteenth chapter occupies a crucial position in Gibbon's history. Knowing when he wrote it that he would have a great deal to relate about the Christian Church in the course of his long narrative, and planning with great care the strategy of his attack, he must have realized that all subsequent investigations of church affairs would depend in great measure on the success of his study of the primitive church. He was the first of the secular historians to venture into this hallowed ground. The primitive church has always been appealed to by Protestants and on occasions by Catholics as the best example of the pure embodiment of Christianity. The primitive church is the fountain-head of the empire of Christ,

[14] ii. 27.

the origin and growth of which is indissolubly connected with the fall of the empire of Rome. Consequently, Gibbon spared no pains in doing his research in this material. One can see in the notes appended to his study and in his *Vindication* a display of erudition which is amazing. His scholarship was so thorough that very few contemporary theologians were able to meet him in the arena which should have been their own.

In the composition of this chapter he had a twofold objective. As a philosophic historian studying one of the most important revolutions of Western culture, he was interested in discovering whatever lessons for posterity this revolution might contain. Believing, as he did, that the effects of other-worldly aspiration, superstition, enthusiasm, and fanaticism were on the whole harmful to mankind, he sought by the most appropriate means available to create doubt as to the validity of a faith which he felt had nourished them. A non-believer himself, he was sure the doubt was justified. But no one can violate with impunity the inner shrine of the temple of faith. A direct attack would do more to alienate his audience than to win them to his side, however right or logical his case might be. Consequently he resorted to irony, and taking the pose of an ingenue in matters of faith, he marshalled a devastating array of facts and proceeded with apparent innocence to raise difficult questions based on them. After reaching his initial objectives he could afford a more outspoken and direct assault, but in the fifteenth chapter he sought only a series of secondary victories which would have a cumulative effect. Little by little he weakens the foundations of faith until the entire temple threatens to come crashing down around our heads. The mind that impels such a relentless attack can afford to win piecemeal. His discussion of each of the five causes for the rapid growth of Christianity contributes in an orderly way to the overwhelming expansion of doubt, a point that will be substantiated by a consideration of his remarks about the second cause.

This was the doctrine of immortality, along with its rewards and punishments. He asserts that the authority and example of Christ were needed for its confirmation; but the way in which he describes the form which the doctrine takes brings into question even the sanction of Divine truth. 'When the promise of eternal happiness was proposed to mankind, on the condition of adopting the faith and of observing the precepts of the gospel, it is no wonder that so advantageous an offer should have been accepted by great numbers. . . .'[15] In brief, the bargain was a good one; but we notice from the first that the doctrine which nature dictated and reason approved is subjected to a limitation. A condition is imposed of adopting the faith and observing the precepts of the gospel, which, at this point in the discussion, might seem an easy and salutary step to take. But the very next matter he mentions is the doctrine of the millennium, an article of faith since regarded as a pious deception. In keeping to the thread of his argument, he relates this doctrine to the rapid spread of Christianity: 'but, as long as, for wise purposes, this error was permitted to subsist in the church, it was productive of the most salutary effects on the faith and practice of Christians'.[16] The reader's suspicions, which are already raised by the assertion that 'the most salutary effects' resulted from falsehood and error, are strengthened and confirmed by the description, which immediately follows, of the New Jerusalem as it was conceived by the early Christians. 'A Garden of Eden, with the amusements of the pastoral life, was no longer suited to the advanced state of society which prevailed under the Roman empire. A city was therefore erected of gold and precious stones, and supernatural plenty of corn and wine was bestowed on the adjacent territory. . . .' He goes on to say that in later years, when the edifice of the Church was almost completed, the doctrine of the millennium, described as a temporary support, was laid aside and rejected as 'the absurd invention of heresy and fanaticism'. Yet the Church suffers in both the acceptance and rejection of this doctrine: in the acceptance because of its bold-faced absurdity; in its rejection, because by admitting the employment of a pious fraud on the part of the early fathers, the Church brings into question the validity of other matters of faith. Gibbon is quick to capitalize on this point: 'The Christian . . . founded his belief much less on the fallacious arguments of reason than on the authority of tradition and the interpretation of scripture',[17] he writes, and the play between reason and authority is fully developed, now that 'the authority of tradition' is partially crippled. This antithesis is followed by an even stronger one. Since the one qualification for bliss in after-life is adopting the

[15] ii. 22–23. [16] ii. 23. [17] ii. 26.

true faith, a logical result is the damnation of the pagan world. One of the best specimens of Gibbon's irony is seen when he writes: 'A charitable hope might, perhaps, be indulged in favour of Socrates, or some other sages of antiquity, who had consulted the light of reason before that of the gospel had arisen.'[18] The men who consulted the light of the gospel unanimously affirmed that those who continued to worship false gods after the birth or crucifixion of Christ would be eternally damned. As might be expected, the paragraph continues with an illustration of the difference between the light of reason, the light of those who interpreted the gospel, and the light of the gospel itself. In a single sentence Gibbon distributes the three into what he considers to be their proper relationship to each other, and here again we have an example of his genius for perspective: 'These rigid sentiments [i.e. the damnation of the pagans], which had been unknown to the ancient world, appear to have infused a spirit of bitterness into a system of love and harmony.'[19]

In such a manner the discussion moves forward like a great tide, with each ironic wave pushing the doubt a bit farther, and then receding as the next wave prepares to break on the shore. In discussing the third cause, the miraculous powers of the primitive church, Gibbon brings into question the whole matter of divine interference with the normal order of the world. The implication here and elsewhere is that all the claims of miracles are at least suspicious, and most probably fraudulent. 'But the miraculous cure of diseases, of the most inveterate or even preternatural kind, can no longer occasion any surprise', he writes, and notice the way he has drawn in his reader, 'when we recollect that in the days of Irenaeus, about the end of the second century, the resurrection of the dead was very far from being esteemed an uncommon event. . . .'[20] A paraphrase would read: we should not be surprised by impossibilities when they are attended or preceded by absurdities.

The invalidation of miracles, we discover, is only a preparation for an ironic climax. This is his definition of faith, which he can now state with precision. He says that the easy acceptance of fraudulent miracles accustomed the early Christians to accept with the same ease, but with more justice, 'the authentic wonders

[18] ii. 26. [19] ii. 27. [20] ii. 29.

of evangelic history'. By this time in the discussion, surely the word 'authentic' is suspect. Gibbon drives home his point: 'and thus miracles that exceeded not the measure of their own experience inspired them with the most lively assurance of mysteries which were acknowledged to surpass the limits of their understanding'.[21] He has one more victory to win, and he pushes his argument towards its climax: 'It is this deep impression of supernatural truths which has been so much celebrated under the name of faith; a state of mind described as the surest pledge of the divine favour and of future felicity, and recommended as the first or perhaps the only merit of a Christian. According to the more rigid doctors, the moral virtues, which may be equally practised by the infidels, are destitute of any value or efficacy in the work of our justification.'[22] Having cast suspicions on both early miracles and the mysteries of the gospel, Gibbon emphasizes the point that absolute belief in them is the first and perhaps the only merit of a Christian; and he places beside this merit the useless virtue of pagans and infidels. Such is his intellectual energy that by means of this comparison, he also makes the transition to a discussion of the morality of the early Christians!

Irony is a terrible weapon, and in the hands of a master like Gibbon it is devastating. If one takes him to task for any remark, he can either parade his authorities, which he does anyway in his footnotes, or remind his critic that he has said nothing impious: it is only human error he is describing. The reasonable questions he raises would seem to deserve reasonable answers, however difficult they may be. He can even point to passages where apparently he has acquiesced in some of the proudest boasts of Christianity. For example, in the matter of conversion of wickedness to virtue, he says: 'The friends of Christianity may acknowledge without a blush that many of the most eminent saints had been before their baptism the most abandoned sinners.'[23] Yet no one will miss the balance of 'most eminent saints' with 'most abandoned sinners'. However complete the conversion, it is difficult to think of superior sanctity emerging from extraordinary wickedness.

His position as the impartial historian enables him to quote the adversaries on either side against each other and produce the exact measure of approbation he wishes. Sometimes this

[21] ii. 31. [22] ii. 31–32. [23] ii. 32.

technique allows him to 'damn with faint praise, assent with civil leer', as in the following example. It is the charge of malice and infidelity, he asserts, that 'the new sect of Christians was almost entirely composed of the dregs of the populace', and he continues to draw out the full arguments of the pagan writers. Then he is able to say: 'This unfavourable picture, though not devoid of a faint resemblance, betrays, by its dark colouring and distorted features, the pencil of an enemy. As the humble faith of Christ diffused itself through the world, it was embraced by *several* persons who derived some consequence from the advantages of nature or fortune.'[24] He continues his narrative by the mention of a few, yet he is forced to admit that the number is still very small, far too small to remove the criticism. Therefore, the ironist seizes the opportunity 'to convert the occasion of scandal into a subject of edification'.[25] By this time the reader should be well aware of the fact that an ironist is never so dangerous as when he offers his service to defend what he is really attacking. The most orthodox Christians must side with Gibbon when he writes: 'Our serious thoughts will suggest to us that the apostles themselves were chosen by providence among the fishermen of Galilee, and that, the lower we depress the temporal condition of the first Christians, the more reason we shall find to admire their merit and success. It is incumbent on us to remember that the kingdom of heaven was promised to the poor in spirit,'—thus far, all is straightforward, or seemingly so; but note the beginning of change in the rest of the sentence: 'and that minds afflicted by calamity and the contempt of mankind cheerfully listen to the divine promise of future happiness; while, on the contrary, the fortunate are satisfied with the possession of this world; and the wise abuse in doubt and dispute their vain superiority of reason and knowledge'.[26] Still, all seems almost above-board, and our reason might grant assent to this remark, even though our suspicions are aroused by the idea of the wise man abusing anything, least of all a superiority of reason and knowledge. We are further suspicious of Gibbon's reasons for calling this superiority vain. Our suspicions are justified, for what we are witnessing is a performance something like that of a delayed-action shell. The shell

[24] ii. 66. Italics mine. [25] ii. 68. [26] Ibid.

enters the edifice much like a harmless dud, but once inside, it explodes with terrible effect.

We stand in need of such reflections to comfort us for the loss of some illustrious characters, which in our eyes might have seemed the most worthy of the heavenly present. The names of Seneca, of the elder and the younger Pliny, of Tacitus, of Plutarch, of Galen, of the slave Epictetus, and of the emperor Marcus Antoninus, adorn the age in which they flourished, and exalt the dignity of human nature. They filled with glory their respective stations, either in active or contemplative life; their excellent understandings were improved by study; Philosophy had purified their minds from the prejudices of the popular superstition; and their days were spent in the pursuit of truth and the practice of virtue. Yet all these sages (it is no less an object of surprise than of concern) overlooked or rejected the perfection of the Christian system. Their language or their silence equally discover their contempt for the growing sect, which in their time had diffused itself over the Roman empire.[27]

This passage climaxes the long chapter which has largely been an *ad hominem* argument. Weakness, poverty, ignorance, and obscurity, are placed disadvantageously beside intellectual power, education, and talent; otherworldly ambitions beside the desire to serve mankind. The reader is left to choose, but Gibbon places the inept apologists for Christianity beside the sages and leaders of Rome. 'In the unskilful hands of Justin and of the succeeding apologists, the sublime meaning of the Hebrew oracles evaporates into distant types, affected conceits, and cold allegories; and even their authenticity was rendered suspicious to an unenlightened Gentile by the mixture of pious forgeries. . . . The adoption of fraud and sophistry in the defence of revelation too often reminds us of the injudicious conduct of those poets who load their *invulnerable* heroes with a useless weight of cumbersome and brittle armour.'[28]

Gibbon has one last point to make, and again it comes in the form of a question: 'How shall we excuse the supine inattention of the Pagan and philosophic world to those evidences which were presented by the hand of Omnipotence, not to their reason, but to their senses?'[29] The question has to do with the miracles of the early Church, the lame walking, the blind seeing, the dead rising,

[27] ii. 68. [28] ii. 69. [29] Ibid.

and especially with the preternatural darkness which accompanied the passion. In an age of science and history this darkness which for three hours covered the world, or at least an important province of the Roman empire, passed altogether without notice. The question Gibbon raises is not answered, of course, except by implication, but I cannot forbear quoting his footnote on how extensive the darkness was. This is the final thrust in the chapter, and I wonder if he could have been thinking of *The Dunciad* when he wrote: 'The fathers, as they are drawn out in battle array by Dom Calmet . . . seem to cover the whole earth with darkness, in which they are followed by most of the moderns.'[30]

Gibbon's use of Socratic irony, although given its most brilliant expression in the fifteenth chapter, can be found in many other parts of the history. The features are the same: the historian professes ignorance, while his subjects boast of extraordinary knowledge or understanding. He will not go where reason cannot go, but he can and does ask those who will venture into the unknown to report their findings. Unlike Socrates, Gibbon is sometimes contemptuous and indignant, and too often those who would explain the mysteries of heaven and hell seem to deserve the language which he reserves for the Gnostics: 'As soon as they launched out into that vast abyss, they delivered themselves to the guidance of a disordered imagination. . . .'[31] The variety he achieves in the application of this technique will be sufficiently illustrated by three examples. The first is drawn from the story of the foundation of Constantinople.

> On foot, with a lance in his hand, the emperor himself led the solemn procession; and directed the line which was traced as the boundary of the destined capital; till the growing circumference was observed with astonishment by the assistants.... 'I shall still advance,' replied Constantine, 'till HE, the invisible guide who marches before me, thinks proper to stop.' Without presuming to investigate the nature or motives of this extraordinary conductor, we shall content ourselves with the more humble task of describing the extent and limits of Constantinople.[32]

The second has to do with a remarkable victory by the Normans over the Arabs:

[30] ii. 70, n. 195. [31] ii. 14. [32] ii. 148.

In the field of Ceramio, fifty thousand horse and foot were overthrown by one hundred and thirty-six Christian soldiers, without reckoning St. George, who fought on horseback in the foremost ranks.[33]

The third is drawn from a later conflict between Christians and Saracens:

'Bear this message,' said Charles, 'to the sultan of Nocera, that God and the sword are umpire between us; and that he shall either send me to paradise, or I will send him to the pit of hell.' The armies met, and, though I am ignorant of Mainfroy's doom in the other world, in this, he lost his friends, his kingdom, and his life, in the bloody battle of Benevento.[34]

The effect varies from serious indignation to pleasant amusement. In the fifteenth chapter there is more than a little indignation, but as the history progresses, this gives way to amusement at folly; and finally the extravagant actions of theological synods and of the partisans in religious controversy deserve to be treated in the mock-heroic vein. Irony here is seen more clearly as the ally of comedy, and the various devices of ridicule and contempt are marshalled for some devastating satire. A literary man with a keen verbal sensitivity, and following at a short distance the footsteps of Swift, Pope, and Fielding, would, after all, be expected to excel in satiric technique. In one place, while speaking of a general antidote to religious credulity, Gibbon praises Hume for seizing the battery and turning the cannon against his enemies. Our discussion so far has shown that this technique is central for Gibbon also. In having the dogmatists speak for themselves either through action or commentary, Gibbon has only to arrange the scene or set the stage. In the councils of Ferrara and Florence, one of the items of dispute was the nature of purgatory, and Gibbon writes, 'whether their souls were purified by elemental fire was a doubtful point, which in a few years might be conveniently settled on the spot by the disputants'.[35]

The comic is further seen in the almost farcical passage concerning Barlaam and the light of Mount Tabor. Disputes about this light consummated the religious follies of the Greeks, Gibbon writes. How the light is discovered is best told in the language of an eleventh-century abbot:

[33] vi. 192. [34] vi. 475. [35] vii. 109.

'When thou art alone in thy cell,' says the ascetic teacher, 'shut thy door, and seat thyself in a corner; raise thy mind above all things vain and transitory; recline thy beard and chin on thy breast; turn thy eyes and thy thoughts towards the middle of thy belly, the region of the navel; and search the place of the heart, the seat of the soul. At first, all will be dark and comfortless; but, if you persevere day and night, you will feel an ineffable joy; and no sooner has the soul discovered the place of the heart than it is involved in a mystic and ethereal light.'[36]

Gibbon brands this kind of vision with the language he feels it deserves: 'the production of a distempered fancy, the creature of an empty stomach and an empty brain', which, none the less, the Quietists adored as the pure and perfect essence of God Himself. But much later in his narrative, when he is discussing the revival of learning in Italy, he has occasion to follow the unfortunate Barlaam who encountered the votaries at Mount Tabor on his return to Greece from Italy. The same Barlaam who had instructed Petrarch and who had been the first to revive the writings of Homer beyond the Alps had the audacity in Greece rashly to provoke 'the swarms of fanatic monks by attempting to substitute the light of reason to that of their navel'.[37] As can be seen, the comedy spreads out from this little anecdote to the age itself.

The mention of swarms of fanatic monks brings us to the object of Gibbon's most savage satire, for they are the extremists about whom he writes: 'The Ascetics, who obeyed and abused the rigid precepts of the gospel, were inspired by the savage enthusiasm which represents man as a criminal and God as a tyrant. They seriously renounced the business, and the pleasures, of the age; abjured the use of wine, of flesh, and of marriage; chastised their body, mortified their affections, and embraced a life of misery, as the price of eternal happiness.'[38] Even the monk Telemachus, who, at the sacrifice of his own life, put a stop to the gladiatorial combats in the amphitheatre, is not allowed the full measure of praise: '[His] death was more useful to mankind than his life',[39] Gibbon says. As the very type of religious enthusiasts, the monks goad Gibbon into exhausting the language of contempt.

From Alexander Pope he may have learned the value of reducing his enemies to the size and form of insects and then

[36] vi. 506. [37] vii. 119. [38] iv. 57. [39] iii. 258.

displaying his own virtuosity in destroying them. Pope asks permission to comment on Sporus:

> Yet let me flap this bug with gilded wings,
> This painted child of Dirt, that stinks and stings;

or he presents his scribblers as spiders, spinning out their slight, self-pleasing threads. The same technique appears in Gibbon. A metaphor presents the official spies of Constantine and his successors as maggots: 'Under the warm influence of a feeble reign, they multiplied to the incredible number of ten thousand. . . .'[40] Sometimes the statement is more direct: 'the number of eunuchs could be compared only with the insects of a summer's day'.[41] Characteristically, the fanatic monks are described as 'swarms', or in a more telling sentence he uses the language which in Exodus describes the plague of locusts, and the monks arising from the Nile, overspread and darken the face of the Christian world. Gibbon echoes Pope very closely when he describes the reading and perhaps the writing of Saint Cyril: 'he extended round his cell the cobwebs of scholastic theology'.[42] The reader is perplexed by the intentional ambiguity as to whether these cobwebs had been spun by Cyril or by other spiders. Variations in the technique are seen in Gibbon's description of the monks of Egypt. At first he groups them with animals: 'posterity might repeat the saying, which had formerly been applied to the sacred animals of the same country, That, in Egypt, it was less difficult to find a god than a man'.[43] The simple antithesis between monks and men prepares the way for further satire, because some of the monks, at any rate, appeared to regret that they had not been born sacred cows: 'They aspired to reduce themselves to the rude and miserable state in which the human brute is scarcely distinguished above his kindred animals; and a numerous sect of Anachorets derived their name from their humble practice of grazing in the fields of Mesopotamia. . . .'[44] They were found in the desert, the pasture, and one, at least, on top of a pillar: 'the name and genius of Simeon Stylites have been immortalized by the singular invention of an aerial penance'.[45]

[40] ii. 188. [41] ii. 420. [42] v. 107.
[43] iv. 60. [44] iv. 73. [45] Ibid.

But however Gibbon wishes to reduce them to the level of noxious insects, in their actions they unhappily escape from that category. Too often we read of their real devastations: 'Jerusalem was occupied by an army of monks; in the name of the one incarnate nature, they pillaged, they burnt, they murdered; the sepulchre of Christ was defiled with blood; and the gates of the city were guarded in tumultuous rebellion against the troops of the emperor.'[46] And there are places where, by a simple grouping of details, such as in the following passage, Gibbon has recourse to the less polite techniques of Swift. 'The priests and monks were the loudest and most active in the destruction of the schismatics; and they chanted a thanksgiving to the Lord, when the head of a Roman cardinal, the pope's legate, was severed from his body, fastened to the tail of a dog, and dragged with savage mockery through the city.'[47] The degree of contempt, indignation, or amusement which Gibbon exacts from his readers is always carefully measured and controlled. He turns the fanatics into insects when they seem to deserve such treatment; at other times, when he wishes us to understand that the insects are capable of the worst crimes, he presents them in life size and suddenly impresses his reader with their power. A summary illustration is found in the religious war which was instituted by Christian sects over the question of the true nature of the Prince of Peace. One hundred thousand Romans were killed and the once fruitful province of Sarmatia was left a desolate and smoking ruin. After the horrors of this narrative have been suitably impressed on his readers, Gibbon reflects on the possible fate of the 'heretics' who were slain in the war. Notice how, in the following quotation, by shifting from the short to the long view he is able again to reduce the fanatics to what he considers their proper size. In so doing, he makes his final commentary on the action, and places it in perfect perspective.

If they [the dead heretics] were already in the fangs of the daemon, their torments could neither be aggravated nor assuaged by human industry. If in the company of saints and angels they enjoyed the rewards of piety, they must have smiled at the idle fury of the theological insects who still crawled on the surface of the earth. The foremost of these insects, the emperor of the Romans [Justinian],

[46] v. 127. [47] vi. 373.

darted his sting, and distilled his venom. . . . The victims were no longer subject to his power, and the vehement style of his edicts could only proclaim their damnation and invite the clergy of the East to join in a full chorus of curses and anathemas.[48]

Not the least of Gibbon's satiric techniques is the transference of terminology. Christianity, as a militant and victorious religion, is described in the language used for military conquest. An awareness of this fact begins in the fifteenth chapter and becomes fully developed before that chapter is concluded. As the history progresses, the language of pagan mythology is added to that of military conquest. Just as Zeus hurled thunderbolts, so the popes hurl their anathemas and excommunications. The spiritual thunders of the Vatican may remind one of a storm over Mount Olympus; the fulminations of the popes, the rages of Jupiter. That the organization of the Church is described like that of the legions who were conquered by it, that the action of the popes should be like that of the gods they unseated can be justified by the age-old practice of assigning the virtues or at least the powers of the vanquished to the victor, and recognizing the victor's excellence in these powers. The satire arises from the fact that the Prince of Peace sought to conquer by love, not the sword; that the god of mercy and forgiveness de-emphasizes his power. In the temptations in the desert, Christ refused the sword and empire of Caesar. And Gibbon justifies the transference of terminology with the remark,

Those who survey, with a curious eye, the revolutions of mankind may observe that the gardens and circus of Nero on the Vatican, which were polluted with the blood of the first Christians, have been rendered still more famous by the triumph and by the abuse of the persecuted religion. On the same spot, a temple, which far surpasses the ancient glories of the Capitol, has been since erected by the Christian Pontiffs, who, deriving their claim of universal dominion from an humble fisherman of Galilee, have succeeded to the throne of the Caesars, given laws to the barbarian conquerors of Rome, and extended their spiritual jurisdiction from the coast of the Baltic to the shores of the Pacific Ocean.[49]

The victors were subdued by the arts of their vanquished rivals,

[48] v. 138. [49] ii. 85–86.

and it is the 'religion of Constantine' that triumphs, according to one of his statements, rather than the religion of Christ.

We find that when he comes to summarize the five causes for the rapid growth and conquest of Christianity, the basic metaphor of the passage is that of a valorous, well-equipped, highly disciplined army. 'It was by the aid of these causes', he writes,

> exclusive zeal, the immediate expectation of another world, the claim of miracles, the practice of rigid virtue, and the constitution of the primitive church, that Christianity spread itself with so much success in the Roman empire. To the first of these, the Christians were indebted for their invincible valour, which disdained to capitulate with the enemy whom they were resolved to vanquish. The three succeeding causes supplied their valour with the most formidable arms. The last of these causes united their courage, directed their arms, and gave their efforts that irresistible weight which even a small band of well-trained and intrepid volunteers has so often possessed over an undisciplined multitude, ignorant of the subject, and careless of the event of the war.[50]

If reason and justice dictate or if his integrity permits, Gibbon will separate a group from its normal background and obtain fresh perspective by giving it a new context. This is done by means of metaphor, as in this example, or by transference of diction, or by contrasting tone. Sometimes the metaphorical separation is intensified by express statement, as in the remark: 'But the patriarch of Alexandria, whilst he darted the thunders of a god, exposed the errors and passions of a mortal. . . .'[51] Or it is done by sudden diminution or magnification of the object under consideration. We can detect the lessons of Swift in Gibbon's remark that, 'In the polemic microscope an atom is enlarged to a monster, and each party was skilful to exaggerate the absurd or impious conclusions that might be extorted from the principles of their adversaries'.[52] The technique is effective because Gibbon himself does not extort, but presents his statements everywhere with the calm assurance and judicious balance which can only result from a sure grasp of knowledge and evidence. Within the bounds of his own philosophy and within his deliberately limited view, he is impartial, and this is the source of his great strength.

[50] ii. 54. [51] v. 113. [52] v. 106.

The technique of separation and arrangement is implemented by other means than those of metaphor and contrasting size. The dignity of tone with which the whole work is delivered must inevitably produce a mock-heroic effect when it is applied to what is mean or petty. In one of the numerous squabbles for the Roman throne, Quintilius came to rule seventeen days. His rights were challenged almost immediately, and note the way the tone and the suggestion of ancient Roman stoicism make ridiculous his subsequent action. 'As soon as he was informed that the great army of the Danube had invested the well-known valour of Aurelian with Imperial power, he sunk under the fame and merit of his rival; and, ordering his veins to be opened, prudently withdrew himself from the unequal contest.'[53] In another passage we have a sentence framed, balanced, and weighed in a way that would be worthy to celebrate a Roman triumph. Gibbon uses it to place the subject beyond contempt: 'The deepest wounds were inflicted on the empire during the minorities of the sons and grandsons of Theodosius; and, after those incapable princes seemed to attain the age of manhood, they abandoned the church to the bishops, the state to the eunuchs, and the provinces to the Barbarians.'[54] As this example illustrates, Gibbon adds to his other techniques the device of categorizing by means of parallel structure in his clauses. Bishops, eunuchs, and barbarians are grouped together as the recipients of the empire, and each comments on the others. Variations of this technique provide the reader with considerable amusement. In describing a fair, Gibbon says it was 'annually dedicated to trade, intemperance, and superstition'.[55] Or he will speak of a pilgrim returning from his journey with 'the chains of St. Peter, the right arm of St. Stephen, and an undoubted picture of the Virgin . . .'.[56] A Gothic prince was 'abandoned to wine, to women, and to rustic sports . . .'.[57] In a final example, the conquerors of some Manichaeans 'punished the innocent and guilty by imprisonment, confiscation, and baptism'.[58]

Burlesque and mockery are found throughout the work in varying degrees as the occasion seems to require. From Fielding he may have learned the value of turning all his characters out

[53] i. 291. [54] iv. 165. [55] iv. 192.
[56] iii. 389. [57] iv. 302. [58] vi. 122.

on the highways, but when applied to bishops this procedure has an unusually entertaining effect: 'The highways of the East were crowded with Homoousian, and Arian, and Semi-Arian, and Eunomian bishops, who struggled to outstrip each other in the holy race; the apartments of the palace resounded with their clamours; and the ears of the prince were assaulted, and perhaps astonished, by the singular mixture of metaphysical argument and passionate invective.'[59] And there is something of *Hudibras* to be found in Gibbon's sentence describing a conflict over the Trisagion which nearly cost the Emperor Anastasius his throne and his life. The reader will recall Butler's lines describing those who,

> Decide all controversies by
> Infallible artillery;
> And prove their doctrine orthodox
> By apostolic blows and knocks.

Gibbon may have been thinking of them when he wrote: 'The Trisagion, with and without this obnoxious addition, was chanted in the cathedral by two adverse choirs, and, when their lungs were exhausted, they had recourse to the more solid arguments of sticks and stones.'[60] Sometimes his irony has the vicious effect of a whip, as the tail of the sentence suddenly snaps back on what has preceded it. Gibbon, who has tried to show the tyranny of the Church, and who has branded Christianity as a sect, writes about the Christian attitude at the death of the Persian, Chosroes. 'According to the faith and mercy of his Christian enemies, he sunk without hope into a still deeper abyss; and it will not be denied that tyrants of every age and sect are the best entitled to such infernal abodes.'[61]

In the next chapter we shall see among other things the finer instruments of Gibbon's satire as they appear in the construction of his sentences and the selection of his diction, but as a final comment on Gibbon's major satiric techniques, we should quote the brilliant and judicious assessment made by another great ironist. Of the art and intentions of Gibbon and Voltaire, Lord Byron says:

[59] iii. 2. [60] v. 131. [61] v. 92–93.

SATIRE

They were gigantic minds, and their steep aim
Was, Titan-like, on daring doubts to pile
Thoughts which should call down thunder, and the flame
Of heaven again assail'd, if Heaven the while
On man and man's research could deign do more than smile.

VII · LANGUAGE

> The attainment of style consists in so knowing words that one will communicate the various parts of what one says with the various degrees and weights of importance which one wishes.
>
> EZRA POUND

GIBBON once said that 'the style of an author should be the image of his mind'. We have already noticed some of the major ideas of Gibbon's mind, and in considering the form and structure of *The Decline and Fall* as well as the narrative and satiric techniques employed by its author, we have seen examples of how his mind functions. In the present chapter I should like to consider the details of his prose style: the structure of his sentences, his use of metaphor and simile, his interest in sounds, and the rhythms of his prose. The homogeneity of the long history is striking; viewed from a distance the epic work has the neatness and order of a great army passing in review. There seems to be a regularity of pace as the narrative marches through decades and centuries. A closer look, however, reveals extraordinary variety in the texture of Gibbon's composition and a gratifying subtlety of movement. The qualities of great prose are here: judiciousness, precision, solidity, clarity, emotional force, and intellectual strength. Variations in rhythm, modulations of tone, aptness of metaphor, and energy of phrasing all contribute to the literary satisfaction of his auditors. Nor is there any question that Gibbon's prose is designed for aural reception. E. M. W. Tillyard, who reports having read aloud more than half of *The Decline and Fall*, can testify on this point.[1] There is an inevitability in the march of Gibbon's long periods; they do not yield to paraphrase. Only at the cost of essential qualities of thought, tone, or emotion can they be rendered in different words. Above all, the prose is the result of magnificent intellectual power which has the

[1] E. M. W. Tillyard, *The English Epic and its Background* (London, 1954), p. 522.

free and able command of one of the richest, if not the richest, of languages.

At this point it will be useful to recall that Gibbon formed the style of *The Decline and Fall* only after a very long apprenticeship in the study of the greatest writers of four different languages: English, French, Latin, and Greek. The reader of the history will discover borrowings from and echoes of Milton, Pope, Shakespeare, Bossuet, Racine, Montaigne, Montesquieu, Voltaire, Tacitus, Cicero, Virgil, Homer, Xenophon, Herodotus, and many others. He will also find phrases, not to mention rhythms, borrowed from the King James' Bible. In Gibbon's apprentice years at Lausanne he practised the art of double translation with the works of Cicero and those of the lesser-known French stylist Vertôt; he read all of Latin literature; and he spoke and wrote French until it became more natural to him than English. On his return to England he corrected this imbalance by a study of English writers, especially Addison, Steele, Pope, and Swift. We have also noted his great admiration of Robertson and Hume, and the diligence with which he applied himself to Greek is characteristic of his linguistic interests. The great literature of Europe went into the making of Gibbon's style, filtered, of course, by the predispositions of his own temperament and growing taste.

That the 'masterly pencil of Tacitus' was the most important influence has long been recognized.[2] Gibbon calls him 'the first of historians who applied the science of philosophy to the study of facts',[3] and again and again throughout *The Decline and Fall* one finds examples of Gibbon's emulation of 'the expressive conciseness' of that disillusioned Roman. Sometimes a statement such as 'Sensit vetus regnandi, falsos in amore, odia non fingere' from the Annals is taken over directly by Gibbon for application in a new context.[4] He greatly admired the 'philosophical' perception, the compression based on a double antithesis, and he sought to achieve a similar strength in his own style. But his appreciation

[2] Shortly after publication of the first volumes of Gibbon's *History* Suzanne Curchod wrote: 'I see Tacitus was the model and perhaps the source of your work. . . .' Quoted by G. M. Young, *Gibbon* (Edinburgh, 1932), p. 133.

[3] *The History of the Decline and Fall of the Roman Empire*, J. B. Bury, ed. (7 vols., London, 1896–1900), i. 213.

[4] '. . . that aged statesman might clearly discern that, however false in friendship, he was sincere in his enmity.' *The Decline and Fall*, vi. 290.

of Voltaire's skill in underlining the incongruous can also be seen in his own sentences as well as on those occasions when he borrows directly from the French historian.[5] And in preceding chapters I have had occasion to refer to the lessons and influence of Milton, Pope, Fielding, Butler, and Swift. When all these names and many more have been mentioned, however, we are still left with Gibbon's own peculiar manner which must finally be recognized as belonging solely to himself.

In forming the style for his great history he consciously set out to build sentences and paragraphs appropriate to his particular subject. 'Many experiments were made before I could hit the middle tone between a dull chronicle and a rhetorical declamation: three times did I compose the first chapter, and twice the second and third, before I was tolerably satisfied with their effect.'[6] The memorial oration on 'the greatest and perhaps the most awful revolution in the history of mankind' demanded no less than did *Paradise Lost* a style all its own. Gibbon's well-defined manner of speaking and the details of his style reflect as clearly as do the thoughts that he expresses his whole attitude towards his subject and, indeed, his whole philosophy of life. His faith in reason and its power to analyse and judge all of life explains the special emphasis he gives to the qualifying words in each sentence. His understanding of the enormous debt of European civilization to the classical world explains why his diction is so Latinate, and because he celebrates the virtues of contemporary Europe his language and his manner are cosmopolitan and urbane. In the balance and proportion, in the parallelism and antitheses of his sentences we see reflected those principles of a rationally ordered existence which give meaning and dignity to human life. Finally, the English language, with its innumerable borrowings from French, Latin, and Greek, was an admirable vehicle of expression for the citizen of enlightened Europe.

Gibbon has commented on his method of composition in his autobiography: 'It has always been my practice to cast a long paragraph in a single mould, to try it by my ear, to deposit it in

[5] '"It is thus", says a lively writer, "that a Christian king died near the ruins of Carthage, waging war against the sectaries of Mahomet, in a land to which Dido had introduced the deities of Syria."' *The Decline and Fall*, vi. 362.

[6] *The Memoirs of the Life of Edward Gibbon*, G. B. Hill, ed. (New York, 1900), p. 190.

my memory, but to suspend the action of the pen till I had given the last polish to my work.'[7] If this is a true description, and there seems to be no reason to doubt that it is, the performance is very impressive, for many paragraphs of *The Decline and Fall* cover several pages. The mind that was able to embrace the vast quantity of material which made up the history would, presumably, have less difficulty in holding all the details of even an unusually long paragraph clearly before it. But however the reader is impressed by the beauty, the strength, and the unity of Gibbon's rolling paragraphs, the best entrance to an understanding of the rhythm and composition of *The Decline and Fall* is to be found in a study of smaller units of his prose.

In its usual form the sentence in Gibbon is a period made up of three or more members. By the time he wrote, the uses of this type of sentence had been fully developed in English and French by a host of writers of the seventeenth and eighteenth centuries, although Johnson and Robertson should be cited as his most immediate predecessors in English.[8] In the hands of Gibbon the periodic sentence is a wonderfully flexible instrument. It provides him with a vast range of opportunities for the varied expression of complex thought. Thousands upon thousands of sentences constructed in a similar fashion might produce intolerable monotony, but Gibbon constantly shifts his emphasis, balances and rebalances his clauses, groups and regroups his ideas. The skilful use of antithesis, the paralleling of ideas, the changes in rhythm all add to the variety of the expression. The structure of the period can be inverted, or suspense can be created as the reader waits for the completion of the thought. Surprise as well as humour often greet the reader as the period draws to a close.

The sharpest edge of Gibbon's mind is seen in the qualifying adverbs and adjectives. By these the subject or the action is given the exact colouring which Gibbon believes it deserves. The appropriateness of the effects he creates will be judged by each reader individually. One may quarrel with this or that effect, but no one can deny that it has been carefully planned. Gibbon is everywhere a conscious and deliberate stylist, one who seeks to write with the

[7] *Memoirs*, p. 201.

[8] See G. M. Young's excellent discussion of Gibbon's indebtedness to Robertson and Johnson, *Gibbon*, pp. 82 ff.

utmost precision and grace. In the details of his style we find the same drive towards clarity and exactitude that we have noticed in its larger features. The mind of Gibbon moves into every area of human experience and pronounces judgement on it all. He has committed himself to the task of commenting upon every relevant detail which is available to the conscientious historian, and the degree of success he achieved in fulfilling this commitment is no less astonishing than the fact that he undertook such an obligation at all.

An example of Gibbon's judgement in operation can be seen in the following pair of sentences taken from the narrative of Quintilius's brief reign:

> Without delay or reflection, he assumed the purple at Aquileia, where he commanded a considerable force;

and,

> though his reign lasted only seventeen days, he had time to obtain the sanction of the senate, and to experience a mutiny of the troops.

> As soon as he was informed that the great army of the Danube had invested the well-known valour of Aurelian with Imperial power, he sunk under the fame and merit of his rival;

and,

> ordering his veins to be opened, prudently withdrew himself from the unequal contest.[9]

Many writers would have said: 'Without delay he assumed the purple', but Gibbon's judgement is expressed in 'Without delay *or reflection*'. It is also characteristic of him to emphasize the ambivalence of Quintilius's act by paralleling the sanction of the senate with the mutiny of the troops. A further judgement is contained in Gibbon's assertion that it is not Aurelian but 'the well-known valour of Aurelian' that is invested with imperial power. The reference to prudence in the last sentence reminds us of the absence of reflection emphasized at the beginning of the quotation. In this case a tardy prudence can be exercised only through a normally imprudent act; and the suicide of Quintilius is accurately represented in the grammatical structure of the sentence

[9] *The Decline and Fall,* i. 291.

by Gibbon's words, 'withdrew himself', instead of 'he withdrew'. Gibbon's final judgement resides in the irony and is further clarified by the elevation of the diction which renders the actions of Quintilius even more ridiculous than they would otherwise seem to be.

I should point out also that each of these sentences can be divided into two major parts, joined by a co-ordinating conjunction. This structure provides Gibbon with another means of commentary beyond the qualifying epithets which one finds so frequently in his sentences, a clarification of the action which emerges from what I should like to call the dualistic or two-part unit of thought. What I am going to say about it should not, indeed cannot, be applied to every sentence or group of sentences in *The Decline and Fall,* but the unit appears so frequently in Gibbon's prose that I am led to believe that it is basic to his thinking and to his expression. It results from his predilection for considering at least two and sometimes three major aspects of a situation simultaneously and not completing his thought until these parts have been brought into clear relationship to each other. The unit is not always confined to the single sentence, although in the sentences cited above it is. There, the relationship between the two parts of each sentence is that of cause and effect. Another example of the same kind of relationship is seen in the following sentence:

> The understandings of their congregation were perplexed by mystery,
> their passions were inflamed by invectives;

and

> they rushed from the Christian temples of Antioch or Alexandria prepared either to suffer or inflict martyrdom.[10]

In other sentences the relationship between the two main parts is often that of comparison or contrast:

> The Olympian Jove, created by the muse of Homer and the chisel of Phidias, might inspire a philosophic mind with momentary devotion;

[10] ii. 327.

but

> these catholic images were faintly and flatly delineated by monkish artists in the last degeneracy of taste and genius.[11]

Sometimes Gibbon will put the specific details in the first part of the sentence and clarify them by a general assertion in the second part:

> The villages and open towns had been abandoned, on their approach by the inhabitants,
> the cattle was driven away,
> the provisions removed or destroyed,
> the bridges broken down,

nor

> was anything left which could afford either shelter or subsistence to an invader.[12]

Sometimes the general assertion comes in the first part and the modifying details follow in the second:

> The form of these religious edifices was simple and oblong;

though

> they might sometimes swell into the shape of a dome, and sometimes branch into the figure of a cross.[13]

In a far more complex example Gibbon shows us what variety he can achieve and still retain the basic dualism of his thought unit. He is describing the Romans under the Emperor Majorian:

> The circus and theatres might still excite, but they seldom gratified, the desires of the people;
> the temples, which had escaped the zeal of the Christians, were no longer inhabited either by gods or men;
> the diminished crowds of the Romans were lost in the immense space of their baths and porticoes;

and

> the stately libraries and halls of justice became useless to an indolent generation, whose repose was seldom disturbed either by study or business.[14]

The main clauses which make up the first part of this sentence

[11] v. 249. [12] i. 183. [13] ii. 321. [14] iv. 19.

describe the relationship between the people of Rome and three kinds of their public buildings. There is a progression from the description of an attitude to the concrete image of immense space and diminished crowds. The second part of the sentence gives us a fourth example, but one which is important enough to contain the significant generalization which Gibbon wishes to make about the Romans of this period. The essence of the sentence consists of a contrast between buildings, which are monuments to the energies and activities of their creators, and the indolence of the present generation. It is, therefore, appropriate that the key image is that of little crowds in a spacious edifice. The image comes almost at the centre, where the two parts of the sentence are joined. The three members which make up the first part of the period build up anticipation, as the reader wonders what use Gibbon intends to make of these details; the second part of the sentence gratifies the anticipation by placing all the details in clear relationship. The reader has come to understand the spiritual poverty of the Romans by a description of their incapacity or unwillingness to use seven kinds of public buildings. No one part of the sentence is complete by itself; the full thought requires all the details. Note also that Gibbon has grouped temples in the same part of the sentence with circus, theatres, baths, and porticoes and given to libraries and halls of justice the dignity of standing by themselves in the more important and emphatic part of the sentence. The 'amusements' of life concern him in the first part of the sentence; the business of life in the second. In both, the Romans are found wanting.

Whatever the relationship between the parts may be, and however varied, the important point to notice is that the key unit of Gibbon's thought is usually composed of two major elements, neither of which is complete without the other. This unit does not always fit the structure of the individual sentence, but sometimes embraces two sentences; sometimes several such units are apparent within a single sentence. In the following example we have two sentences held together as a single thought by the contrast between a supposition and a reality. The thought is not completed until the facts are brought to bear on the supposition. The transitional words which join the contrasting parts are shown in italic type.

> A speculative reasoner might suppose that their faith had a strong and serious influence on their practice; and that the soldiers of the cross, the deliverers of the holy sepulchre, prepared themselves by a sober and virtuous life for the daily contemplation of martyrdom. *Experience blows away this charitable illusion; and* seldom does the history of profane war display such scenes of intemperance and prostitution as were exhibited under the walls of Antioch.[15]

Rather than moving from one assertion to another, Gibbon's prose expresses a series of relationships. He will play the general against the specific, the illusion against the reality, effect will grow out of cause, reaction out of action. Although the relationship is usually between only two parts, sometimes the reader finds three main elements. The three-part units are usually found at the end of paragraphs or at the end of chapters:

> Like hounds, or hawks, who had strayed from the lawful owner, they might be lost and claimed;
> the slave and falcon were of the same value;

but

> three slaves, or twelve oxen, were accumulated to equal the price of the war-horse;

and

> a sum of three hundred pieces of gold was fixed, in the age of chivalry, as the equivalent of the more noble animal.[16]

Gibbon narrates, comments, evaluates, and judges as he goes along; the dualistic unit of his prose is admirably suited to the multiplicity of his artistic intentions, for it enables him to tell the reader what is happening and how he should feel about it all at the same time. Among other advantages, this instrument enables Gibbon to place the emphasis exactly where he wants it with more precision than he could otherwise achieve. In the periodic sentence the emphasis normally comes at the very end, as the thought is completed. Gibbon often uses the termination of his period as the occasion for humour:

> . . . his ignorance of art and language was compensated by sighs and tears and ejaculations;

[15] vi. 302. [16] vi. 321.

and

> Peter supplied the deficiency of reason by loud and frequent appeals to Christ and his mother, to the saints and angels of Paradise, with whom he had personally conversed.[17]

But the dualistic unit provides Gibbon with another point of emphasis at the beginning of the second part of the unit. In the following example he wishes to emphasize the word 'merit'; he builds up to it by clauses which elevate the reader to the point where he anticipates the completion of the thought, and then comes the word 'merit' with enough emphasis to parallel in importance 'the free voices of an enlightened people'.

> The genius of the founders still lived in those venerable seats;
> the ambition of succeeding to the masters of human reason excited a generous emulation;

and

> the merit of the candidates was determined, on each vacancy, by the free voices of an enlightened people.[18]

In describing the actions of Belisarius he emphasizes the impact of the arms of the hero on the enemy. The first three clauses build up the power, which is then released on the Goths. They flee, and we are left at the end of the unit with the figure of the hero. The energy is released and expended altogether on the Goths.

> The Roman general was strong, active, and dexterous;
> on every side he discharged his weighty and mortal strokes;
> his faithful guards imitated his valour and defended his person;

and

> the Goths, after the loss of a thousand men, fled before the arms of an hero.[19]

When action is rapid the parts of Gibbon's thought unit are shortened, and the break between them sometimes comes in the middle of a sentence to produce the more rapid flow of narrative:

> They were rashly pursued to their camp;

[17] vi. 260. [18] iv. 263. [19] iv. 313.

and

the Romans, oppressed by multitudes, made a gradual, and at length precipitate, retreat to the gates of the city;

the gates were shut against the fugitives;

and

the public terror was increased by the report that Belisarius was slain.

His countenance was indeed disfigured by sweat, dust, and blood;
his voice was hoarse,
his strength was almost exhausted;

but

his unconquerable spirit remained;

he imparted that spirit to his desponding companions;

and

their last desperate charge was felt by the flying Barbarians, as if a new army, vigorous and entire, had been poured from the city.

The Flaminian gate was thrown open to a *real* triumph;

but

it was not before Belisarius had visited every post, and provided for the public safety, that he could be persuaded by his wife and friends to taste the needful refreshments of food and sleep.

In the more improved state of the art of war, a general is seldom required, or even permitted, to display the personal prowess of a soldier;

and

the example of Belisarius may be added to the rare examples of Henry IV, of Pyrrhus, and of Alexander.[20]

In addition to Gibbon's achieving emphasis and accelerating or retarding movement by balancing the short against the long, or shifting the weight from one member of the thought to the beginning of the next, there is the practice, which is often a source of humour, of emphasizing by means of surprise. The first part of the thought arouses the reader's expectations; the completion of the thought, sometimes the final word, gratifies them, not always

[20] iv. 313.

in the manner expected, but always with a sense of fulfilment. For example:

> The vague commerce of Theodora, and the most detestable precautions, preserved her from the danger which she feared;

yet

> once, and once only, she became a mother.[21]

The build up of passion in the following example is the source of some amusement when Gibbon completes the thought by mentioning the object of that passion. Notice, too, how the length and rhythm of Gibbon's phrases are arranged to provide full release for the passion with the words 'threw herself'. This effect is aided by his omission of the usual copula, and the first major part ends on the words 'honourable love'. The relationship of the two parts is that of cause and effect.

> But the fair Honoria had no sooner attained the sixteenth year of her age than she detested the importunate greatness which must for ever exclude her from the comforts of honourable love;
> in the midst of vain and unsatisfactory pomp, Honoria sighed, yielded to the impulse of nature,
> and threw herself into the arms of her chamberlain Eugenius.[22]

The latitude of these basic units provides Gibbon with ample scope for directing and controlling the movement and energy of his prose; it is also capable of creating more energy than would be possible in a single assertion. In a descriptive section of the history he writes:

> In the heat of the action, seventy men who held the bridle of her camel were successively killed or wounded;

and

> the cage or litter in which she sat was stuck with javelins and darts like the quills of a porcupine.[23]

We see two major features of a single scene. The loss of seventy men gives us one standard by which to measure the intensity of the action; the appearance of the litter after the battle gives us another. The same intensification can be seen in the following

[21] iv. 214. [22] iii. 456. [23] v. 387.

unit, in which we have the action of one man, the judgement of monks on his action, and Gibbon's judgement of both the man and the monks, in the phrase 'the only virtue of his reign'.

> Nicephorus allowed a general liberty of speech and practice;

and

> the only virtue of his reign is accused by the monks as the cause of his temporal and eternal perdition.[24]

The basic units of Gibbon's prose are above all fine and delicate instruments of judgement. They are primarily designed to express a relationship, the perception of which is, after all, the essence of judgement. By comparison and contrast, by shifting emphasis, by variations in length and rhythm, the writer can present a very exact assessment of any subject under consideration. The judgement often is implied by the commentary of one part on the other. Sometimes, as in the following example, it is quite explicit in each part, but the two parts taken together are contrasted and a further judgement is implied.

> The opinions of Arianism might satisfy a cold and speculative mind;

but

> the doctrine of the Nicene Creed, most powerfully recommended by the merits of faith and devotion, was much better adapted to become popular and successful in a believing age.[25]

It is also true that irony, which consists of the measurement of one element against another, has an admirable tool in the dualistic units of Gibbon's thought.

The deadly monotony which would result from an endless parade of sentences each breaking into two or three parts is avoided by the kinds of variety I have already indicated, and the fundamental unit of Gibbon's prose does no more to convert his Pegasus into a rocking-horse than did the couplet to the poetry of Pope. The movement of the prose is made to fit the sense of the action being described. Surprise endings, shifts in tone, variations in length of parts and of the whole, and variations in the kinds of relationship examined, all contribute to the richness and intellec-

[24] v. 278. [25] iii. 148.

tual excitement. Finally, and most important of all, the dualistic unit is the perfect instrument for the two great activities of Gibbon's mind, dissection and creation; in atomizing and discriminating, the dualistic unit also puts together and fuses in new perspective. Ernst Cassirer, writing on 'The Mind of the Enlightenment', shows us how truly representative of its age Gibbon's mind is. Reason, in the whole eighteenth century, Cassirer says, was understood 'not as a sound body of knowledge, principles, and truths, but as a kind of energy, a force which is fully comprehensible only in its agency and effects'.[26] The nature of reason and its power can be understood by its function, he continues: 'And its most important function consists in its power to bind and to dissolve. It dissolves everything merely factual... and everything believed on the evidence of revelation, tradition, and authority.... Following this work of dissolution begins the work of construction. Reason cannot stop with the dispersed parts; it has to build from them a new structure, a true whole.'[27] In fashioning a dualistic unit as the basic means of expression for his long history Gibbon has created a vehicle for the free function of reason in its double, and in this case simultaneous, activity of dissolving and binding.

In forming this unit, Gibbon may have been influenced by the heroic couplet, especially the closed couplet. A clue to the importance of such a possibility is seen in the fact that when he comments on his own style, he uses the terms which, in the eighteenth century, were almost always applied to the couplet: 'The style of the first volume is, in my opinion, somewhat crude and elaborate; and in the second and third, it is ripened into ease, correctness, and numbers. . . .'[28] Certainly the balance and antithesis, the frequent use of comparison and contrast, which mark so much of Gibbon's writing, suggest emulation in the looser medium of prose of some of the artistic techniques found so frequently in the iambic pentameter couplets of the Augustan age.

As a final example of Gibbon's use of the dualistic unit or, perhaps I should say, prose couplet, I should like to quote an entire paragraph (selected, I might add, at random). In it there

[26] *Philosophy of the Enlightenment*, F. C. A. Koelin and J. P. Pettegrove, trans. (Princeton, 1951), pp. 13–14.

[27] Ibid.

[28] *Memoirs*, p. 224.

are four units. The first consists of a simple statement of Trajan's ambition coupled with a 'philosophic' observation about man's desire for military glory. The relationship is between the particular and the general. The second unit consists first of the statement that Trajan's ambition sprang from the desire to emulate Alexander and secondly of the fact that his advanced age made success improbable. The relationship here is between a hope and a reality. The third unit consists of a catalogue of Trajan's successes presented in five consecutive assertions which prepare for the second part of the unit, the effect of these conquests on the spirit of the general. The last unit in the paragraph consists of three parts. Gibbon shifts the point of view back to the senate. In the first part we hear the news received by the Romans and see their rising hopes; in the second we get the fact of Trajan's death; and in the third is expressed the fear that all of his conquests have been in vain and have created new difficulties for the senate. The death of Trajan is made significant for us by Gibbon's placing it in clear relation to the hope which preceded and the fear that followed this event.

Trajan was ambitious of fame;

and

as long as mankind shall continue to bestow more liberal applause on their destroyers than on their benefactors, the thirst of military glory will ever be the vice of the most exalted characters.

The praises of Alexander, transmitted by a succession of poets and historians, had kindled a dangerous emulation in the mind of Trajan. Like him the Roman emperor undertook an expedition against the nations of the east,

but

he lamented with a sigh that his advanced age scarcely left him any hopes of equaling the renown of the son of Philip.

Yet the success of Trajan, however transient, was rapid and specious. The degenerate Parthians, broken by intestine discord, fled before his arms. He descended the river Tigris in triumph, from the mountains of Armenia to the Persian gulf. He enjoyed the honour of being the first, as he was the last of the Roman generals, who ever navigated that remote sea. His fleets ravaged the coasts of Arabia;

and

> Trajan vainly flattered himself that he was approaching towards the confines of India.

> Every day the astonished senate received the intelligence of new names and new nations that acknowledged his sway. They were informed that the kings of Bosphorus, Colchos, Iberia, Albania, Osrhoerne, and even the Parthian monarch himself, had accepted their diadems from the hands of the emperor; that the independent tribes of the Median and Carduchian hills had implored his protection; and that the rich countries of Armenia, Mesopotamia and Assyria were reduced into the state of provinces.

But

> the death of Trajan soon clouded the splendid prospect;

and

> it was justly to be dreaded, that so many distant nations would throw off the unaccustomed yoke, when they were no longer restrained by the powerful hand which had imposed it.[29]

I should point out that what I have been saying about the basic dualism of Gibbon's thought units does not apply to the first and last paragraphs of *The Decline and Fall*. The reason is obvious when one recalls that the first paragraph is a statement of the proposition of the entire history and the last paragraph is Gibbon's peroration. I should also stress the point that one will find many instances in *The Decline and Fall* where the thought is not dualistic, but what I have been trying to describe is the basic movement of the mind, a movement which is varied frequently in its specific manifestations, just as in good poetry we find changes in rhythm from line to line.

A still closer look at the texture of Gibbon's prose will bring us nearer to an appreciation of the mind that was grand in its perception of the vast sweep of history, yet never dozed while considering the most minute details of composition. The active intelligence of Gibbon is as apparent in the construction of the clause as it is in the arrangement of the dominant features of his narrative. It is the mind of an artist who loves language and is fascinated with the myriad effects which can be produced by

[29] i. 6.

careful manipulation of words. Like the connoisseur of fine wines, he savours and tastes; he rolls his phrases around on his palate, and only when fully satisfied with their quality does he present them to his reader. His delight in verbal harmonies is such that the kinds and number of effects the expert practitioner is able to achieve can only be hinted at.

The frequent and varied use of balance and antithesis is an important feature of his style. Like other techniques it contributes to the clarity. As examples, 'the rigid system . . . has been entertained with public applause and secret reluctance',[30] and 'Theodoric loved the virtues which he possessed, and the talents of which he was destitute',[31] are typical of the mind that wished to fix with some exactitude the ambivalence in human affairs. Frequently antithesis is the basis for Gibbon's humour, as we see in his note on Augustine's *Civitate Dei*: 'His learning is too often borrowed; his arguments are too often his own.'[32] Another example is found in his pleasant remarks about the younger Gordian: 'Twenty-two acknowledged concubines and a library of sixty-two thousand volumes attested the variety of his inclinations; and from the productions which he left behind him, it appears that both the one and the other were designed for use rather than ostentation.'[33] Parallel structure is used by Gibbon to contribute to the irony of his work: 'the sons of Constantine seemed impatient to convince mankind that they were incapable of contenting themselves with the dominions which they were unqualified to govern'.[34] Sometimes Gibbon will heap up clauses for emphasis, in this case to impress his reader with the full horror of an evil career. Of John of Cappadocia he writes: '. . . his aspiring fortune was raised on the death of thousands, the poverty of millions, the ruin of cities, and the desolation of provinces'.[35] In other instances parallelism is a means of surprise and often humour because of a single incongruity: 'The count Arcadius indulged the zeal, applauded the eloquence, and neglected the advice of Synesius.'[36] An example of more subtle parallelism and a sharper, more humorous thrust is seen in the careful balancing of opposites in the following sentence: 'The Goths', he writes, 'imperiously demanded that the grandson of Theodoric should

[30] iii. 407. [31] iv. 189. [32] iii. 211, n. 86. [33] i. 176.
[34] ii. 231. [35] iv. 240–1. [36] iii. 247.

be rescued from the dastardly discipline of women and pedants and educated like a valient Goth, in the society of his equals and the glorious ignorance of his ancestors.'[37] The irony and humour which result from Gibbon's use of balance and antithesis, comparison and contrast, are fully justified in the history which studies greatness and littleness, prosperity and decay, and virtue and vice.

In addition to Gibbon's care for the design of his prose and the rhythm of its movement, his concern for the sound of his diction is important. We know that he tried out his paragraphs on his own ear before committing them to paper, and he seems to have taken to heart Pope's precept that 'The sound must seem an Echo to the sense'. Surely the long hiss which is the sound of the following sentence is not an accident. In addition to the evidence of the sentence itself, we know very well how he feels about the men who voluntarily submitted themselves to ecclesiastical rule.

> In the dissolution of the Lombard kingdom, the inhabitants of the duchy of Spoleto sought a refuge from the storm, shaved their heads after the Roman fashion, declared themselves the servants and subjects of St. Peter, and completed by this voluntary surrender, the present circle of the ecclesiastical state.[38]

As we reach the emphatic section of the first part of the sentence, the hiss gives way to an unpleasant combination of *s* and *t* and *p*. The main emphasis of the period falls on the last two words, which are, indeed, spat out by the combination of *s* and *t*.

So often in Gibbon does one find careful and deliberate patterning of sounds to fit the sense that one more example should be cited. The first part of the following quotation uses *s* and *z* sounds to emphasize the slumber of the philosopher; the second part reveals amazing virtuosity in Gibbon's use of *g* sounds to illustrate the ugliness of the avarice.

> . . . he contrasts the innocent repose of a philosopher who sometimes resigned the hours of business to slumber, perhaps to study, with the interested diligence of a rapacious minister, indefatigable in the pursuit of unjust and sacrilegious gain.[39]

In this sentence one finds parallel construction, but with a significant difference. The phrase 'innocent repose of the philosopher'

[37] iv. 302. [38] v. 272. [39] iii. 283.

contains eleven syllables, whereas 'interested diligence of a rapacious minister' contains fifteen. The language used to describe the minister moves much faster than that for the philosopher, and the six syllables of 'indefatigable' suggest how energetic the activities of greed really are. In writing the last part of the sentence Gibbon might have said, 'indefatigable in the pursuit of dishonest gain', but we have only to try to change his sentences to discover how much would be lost by our alterations. The phrase 'pursuit of unjust and sacrilegious gain' emphasizes with each of its five major beats the ugly nature of the minister's crimes.

In all the examples cited so far there is a remarkable concreteness in language. The vague, the blurred, the indefinite are eliminated as he continuously modifies, qualifies, and discriminates with exactness. His interest in concreteness leads to the repeated use of metaphors and similes. His figures of speech are usually unobtrusive, simple, dignified, and apt. They rescue the thought and emotion from abstraction, and, as is always the case in good writing, they call attention more to the equivalence they are designed to illuminate than to the ingenuity which discovered it. Leo IV, whom Gibbon calls a born Roman, 'stood erect like one of the firm and lofty columns that rear their heads above the fragments of the Roman Forum'.[40] In another example the enthusiasm preceding the crusades is explained: 'a new spirit had arisen of religious chivalry and papal dominion, a nerve was touched of exquisite feeling; and the sensation vibrated to the heart of Europe'.[41] Gibbon will explain a significant change in the attitude or ability of large numbers of people by the stylized representation of a single concrete action: 'The heavy weapons of their ancestors, the short sword and the formidable *pilum,* which had subdued the world, insensibly dropped from their feeble hands.'[42] He has many stock metaphors, such as 'the slumber of orthodoxy', 'the yoke of the gospel', 'the silken web of luxury', and 'the ancient fabric of Roman superstition', each one of which increases the concreteness and derives freshness from the variety of uses to which it is put. Simple personification also occurs frequently. In the following sentence it underlines the absurdity of the miracle. The tone is pleasantly humorous as one thinks of walls imitating more illustrious members of their species. The adverb *instantly*

[40] vi. 41. [41] vi. 258. [42] iii. 187.

further contributes to the fun: 'At the sound of his trumpet the walls of the city imitated the example of Jericho and instantly fell to the ground: a splendid miracle which may be reduced to the supposition that some clerical engineers had secretly undermined the foundations of the rampart.'[43] Graceful and apt use of classical allusions is another means by which the actions occurring in the semi-darkness of the distant past are illuminated for us. In describing the march of the troops of Alaric down the Flaminian Way and into the plains of Umbria prior to their sack of Rome, Gibbon pauses to observe that 'they might wantonly slaughter and devour the milk-white oxen, which had been so long reserved for the use of Roman triumphs'.[44] And the crimes and calamities which beset the house of Constantine are compared by Gibbon to those 'the tragic poets have deplored in the devoted lines of Pelops and of Cadmus'.[45] The classical allusions, metaphors, the use of personification sharpen the focus without preoccupying the reader with excessive detail. When the metaphor does call attention to itself it is either for purposes of literary amusement or because the subject being described is unrealizable in any other terms. Gibbon entertains the reader with 'this fictitious deed was transpierced by the pen of Laurentius Valla',[46] and he describes a venture into the unknown with 'the road to paradise, a bridge as sharp as a razor, was suspended over the abyss by the master-hand of the theological artist'.[47]

Coleridge once said that when reading *The Decline and Fall* he felt as though he were 'looking through a luminous haze or fog:—figures come and go, I know not how or why'. But a sentence such as the following emerges from the darkness of the past with a remarkable clarity. We see and understand only what Gibbon wants us to see. Coleridge has missed, or at least not emphasized the fact, that what we do see is etched clearly, sharply, and unmistakably.

After every satisfaction and security had been given, which justice or even delicacy could require, the primate proceeded, by slow journeys, through the provinces of Thrace, Asia, and Syria; and his progress was marked by the abject homage of oriental bishops, who excited his contempt without deceiving his penetration.[48]

[43] iv. 117. [44] iii. 288. [45] ii. 206.
[46] v. 275. [47] v. 126. [48] ii. 370.

The specific details are fashioned in such a way as to stand out solidly by themselves: 'satisfaction and security', 'justice or even delicacy', 'slow journeys', 'Thrace, Asia, and Syria', 'excited his contempt without deceiving his penetration', these phrases make the intangible concrete. The sentence is like a bridge thrown across a black chasm. The metaphor that his progress was 'marked' by abject homage increases the concreteness. The minute details of what specifically constituted the satisfaction and security are omitted, and Gibbon is contented merely to fix the nature or quality of the satisfaction with the modifying phrase. Although he often implies much more than he states, even the implications, one realizes, are subject to careful limitation and control. His prose does not send the mind wandering into the infinite, but rather directs every part of the mind's response.

Some writers have criticized Gibbon for an excessive use of stock diction. Like any other writer of a long prose narrative, Gibbon has favourite words, and he gives his characters standard gestures and responses, which recur again and again in his sentences. The mind is 'inflamed' by ambition, pride is 'soothed' by honours, individuals are 'seduced' by cheerfulness or by 'the dextrous application of gifts and flattery'. Resolutions and alliances are 'embraced', characters frequently 'indulge ambitious hopes', and rashness is usually 'chastised'. Barbarians are 'capriciously impelled by interest or passion', and they 'press forward with vain and thoughtless ardour'. 'Trembling natives relinquish with a sigh the inheritance of their fathers.' Prudence or pride is 'content with extorting', and liberality is sometimes 'profuse' and sometimes 'generous' (i.e. noble). 'Indiscriminate clemency' multiplies enemies, and 'amiable qualities' sometimes degenerate through 'excessive levity'. But it is an unprofitable and unfair exercise to extract stock diction in this way, removing it from its proper context. To do so is to display a few of the outer garments of the prose and to forget the man who wears them. If these words and phrases are returned to the complex and varied sentences from which they are taken the reader will discover that the creative energy of Gibbon has invested them with freshness and vitality, and that the variety of his prose is such that his diction seems stock only to a superficial reader.

One could illustrate indefinitely the striking effects Gibbon achieves, but since the major features of his prose have been suggested, I may be permitted to turn to a final example. It is a beautiful and very moving passage on the fate of the Vandals in Africa, and it will illustrate how perfectly he disciplines and organizes for his purpose every aspect of the thought and emotion which properly belong to the subject he is presenting. The passage follows Gibbon's narrative of the defeat of the Vandals by Belisarius:

> Africa had been their empire, it became their prison; nor could they entertain an hope, or even a wish, of returning to the banks of the Elbe, where their brethren, of a spirit less adventurous, still wandered in their native forests. It was impossible for cowards to surmount the barriers of unknown seas and hostile Barbarians; it was impossible for brave men to expose their nakedness and defeat before the eyes of their countrymen, to describe the kingdom which they had lost, and to claim a share of the humble inheritance which, in a happier hour, they had almost unanimously renounced.[49]

The overwhelming sense of regret which Gibbon manages to capture in this passage should disprove the glib commentators who find him cold and unfeeling, a man without compassion and incapable of empathy; for surely what makes this passage so moving is his ability to project himself into the minds of the defeated and exiled Vandals, who sit on the shores of unknown seas and think of the homeland which is lost to them for ever. The rhythm is slow and funereal. The short phrases of the first sentence emphasize the intentionally heavy, slow beat. The first part of this sentence states simply the naked fact of their imprisonment. The second and much longer half expands the hopelessness of their plight. The next sentence, which shows the reader the fate of all the Vandals by presenting the thoughts of men at both ends of the spectrum of courage, is made up of much longer clauses, and the utter despair is more completely realized. Gibbon discusses the plight of cowards in one long clause; three clauses are required to subdue the spirits of the brave and reconcile them to the inevitability of their doom. In the texture of the passage we note how Gibbon makes the emotion concrete by an unobtrusive use of common metaphor: Africa becomes a prison; unknown

[49] iv. 295.

seas and hostile barbarians are barriers; their defeat as well as their nakedness would be exposed to the eyes of their countrymen. The vowels in the sentence are frequently *o* and *u* in key places, and the consonants are often *n* and *m*, producing a sound of lamentation emphasized in the close of the period: 'they had almost unanimously renounced'. The metre may have the latitude of prose, but the tone, the rhythm, and the spirit are those of the poetic elegy, and the desolation is made complete by the memory of a happier hour at the moment of utter despair.

VIII · CONCLUSION

MY study of the conception and the execution of *The Decline and Fall* has reached a point where an assessment of Gibbon's great achievement may be attempted. As a single, magnificent historical study, the work is incomparable. Other historians, such as Arnold Toynbee, have covered larger subjects, but their work has not the artistic excellence of Gibbon's *Rome*. Modern scientific history bears less the stamp of the author's personality, but the comprehensive mind of Gibbon more than offsets any weakness resulting from personal bias. Artistically engaging re-creations of the past, such as Macaulay's famous chapter on England at the eve of the Glorious Revolution, or Carlyle's *French Revolution*, lack the breadth and scope of *The Decline and Fall*. Moreover, no one has succeeded as has Gibbon in his effort to make an epic of an historical study. Among English writers, at least, Gibbon occupies a position in relation to historians similar to that held by Milton in relation to English poets.

Albert North Whitehead once said that 'So far as European civilization is concerned, the key to history is a comprehension of Rome and the work of its empire',[1] an evident truth to Gibbon who set before himself the immense task of giving his age just such a comprehension. In a study of the fall of Rome and the subsequent recovery of the values of classical civilization he tried to illustrate a great secular truth to his age: that man can achieve his destiny only under conditions of freedom. His belief that man can civilize himself without the aid of super-terrestrial powers and his faith in the value of strenuous liberty form the base for his work; his representation of fourteen centuries in the light of these convictions constitutes his humanistic achievement. To the fall of Rome Gibbon might have applied the agonized lines of Milton's Samson:

> ... what more oft in nations grown corrupt,
> And by their vices brought to servitude,

[1] *The Aims of Education* (New York, 1929), p. 74.

Than to love bondage more than liberty,
Bondage with ease than strenuous liberty.[2]

The responsibilities of man are the result of his being a creature capable of reason, and the cost in blood and suffering which follows his abdication of responsible freedom is held out as a terrible lesson. The pages of *The Decline and Fall* also affirm Gibbon's faith that man is progressing slowly towards the perfection of his own nature through the development of his reason and by the consequent rational ordering of his life. The organizing principle of the work is the decline and fall of one culture; but in Gibbon's understandings of the causes of the fall, we find affirmations of the values and justifications of the bases of the new culture which phoenix-like sprang from the ashes of the old. In this sense *The Decline and Fall* may be called the epic of the Enlightenment, for it celebrates the triumph of human reason in Gibbon's 'philosophic' age. That the work was written in the closing years of the eighteenth century just prior to the great revolutionary shocks which were to change the whole complexion of Europe is an irony at which even Gibbon would smile. But he might point out that such appears to be a condition of epic composition. Certainly the *Aeneid* and *Paradise Lost* were written in periods when the world view they celebrate had already begun to fade.

In a recent study of the English epic, E. M. W. Tillyard has anticipated some of my arguments. His conclusion should be quoted: 'It would be vain to argue that Gibbon was epic in the manner of Langland or Milton. History in a strict sense can never be more than partial epic. It must ever yield much to the pressure of facts; and the battle for unity must always be fought against odds. Gibbon fought that battle as well as a man can; and his history, restricted though it may be as literature, is yet the one English work that expresses the temper of eighteenth century Britain in the age of Hume in something of an epic manner.'[3] As my discussion has shown, I am prepared to go farther than Mr. Tillyard and to assert not only that Gibbon conceived of his history in terms of the epic, but also that despite the pressure of a great mass of facts, he was able to find in the enormous pageant

[2] *Samson Agonistes*, ll. 268–71.

[3] *The English Epic and its Background* (London, 1954), p. 527.

of human affairs an argument which gave a unity to the whole and to all of the parts of the work.

According to Mr. Tillyard, the spirit of the epic may be defined by four main features. The first is the matter of high seriousness and high quality. Certainly the dignity of Gibbon's theme and his distinguished use of language are well suited to this requirement. The second feature is amplitude: the epic must embrace a large area of human experience, but it cannot tolerate 'an undifferentiated and unorganized display of life's many phenomena'.[4] It must harmonize and unify the experience it does include. In addition to what has been said already about the bases for Gibbon's interpretation of an enormous span of history and about the manner in which this experience is patterned, I should stress the fact that amplitude is apparent not only in the great temporal and spatial range of *The Decline and Fall* but also in the multifarious kinds of human experience described. The meanest peasant and the most powerful emperor have a place in its pages, and the full range of human nature is explored. The variety of situations is considerable. Yet all this material is subjected to the shaping power of Gibbon's imagination and judged by the wisdom of his capacious mind. In content as well as in form there is balance and harmony to be found in all the parts.

The structural ideal, and here we are coming to the third characteristic of the epic, has been explained by Mr. Tillyard as follows: '. . . the whole, however long, should remain fluid and unset till the last word has been written, . . . the writer should have everything simultaneously in mind and keep it open to modification throughout the process of composition'.[5] He goes on to say that no man has the powers of memory and control to fulfil the ideal, but mention of it emphasizes a quality in the epic which can result only from the author's keeping the whole suspended in his mind until his composition is complete: the world of the epic must be a thoroughly consistent world. The creation of such a world and its continued realization throughout the long work require an enormous effort of the will. In applying this structural ideal to Gibbon we have noticed that even though he published parts of his history before all of it was composed, although he evolved the long narrative over twenty years of creative labour,

[4] Ibid., p. 8.   [5] Ibid., p. 9.

he was able to sustain the imaginative realization of a unified, consistent, and coherent whole. The world of Gibbon's history is the same whether we visit his representation of Rome in the age of the Antonines, or follow him to the wilds of Tartary or to the banks of the Ganges. The stopping places which Gibbon planned for himself are mere pauses in the total experience of the history, and when the reader arrives at the peroration, then, and only then, does the structure of the work become fixed. At the end of the first and the beginning of the second parts of *The Decline and Fall,* when Gibbon pauses to outline the plans for his last two volumes, we have an example of such a stopping place; but Gibbon's unifying efforts here and especially in the last chapter of his history are so strong that the reader is made to realize that however complete the parts may appear, the larger structure remains fluid and is not set until the very end.

As Mr. Tillyard has observed, the tremendous effort of will required to order the vast amount of material of the epic is more than an external driving force. Its very existence rests on the implicit faith of the artist in the significance of man's efforts to harmonize the apparent chaos of life. Such effort of will is fed by the life-blood of the writer, and not the least of the ways in which Gibbon asserted the dignity and importance of man was in the creation of such form and order as one finds in *The Decline and Fall.* The mind that embraces almost every kind of human experience, that sets each experience in clear relationship to all the others, and judges it by the accumulated wisdom of the ages is itself the best testament to its own worth.

The final qualification for the epic, its choric function, needs little comment. It has often been said that the epic is a cathedral in which are enshrined the ideals and values of a culture, that the writer of the epic is the spokesman for a large group of people living in or near his own time. Gibbon is quite explicitly the spokesman for his age in the numerous reflections—political, moral, and philosophical—with which he studs his narrative. His frequent appeals to the reason and judgement of his contemporaries and his confidence in their ready acceptance of his assertions suggest that he was quite consciously playing the role of spokesman for his times. Moreover, he frequently expatiates with pleasure on the merits of this period. 'Europe is now divided into twelve powerful, though unequal kingdoms, three respectable commonwealths, and a variety of smaller, though independent, states; the chances of royal and ministerial talents are multiplied, at least with the number of its rulers; and a Julian, or Semiramis, may reign in the North, while Arcadius and Honorius again slumber on the thrones of the South. The abuses of tyranny are restrained by the mutual influence of fear and shame; republics have acquired order and stability; monarchies have imbibed the principles of freedom, or, at least, of moderation; and some sense of honour and justice is introduced into the most defective constitutions by the general manners of the times.'[6]

But the modern reader is compelled to pause here, for he lives in a century which has seen Western culture shaken to its very foundations by disastrous wars, and even threatened with extinction, by man's inability to discipline himself and subject his fierce and terrible passions to the control of reason. Twentieth-century man instinctively rebels at what appears to be the complacent optimism with which Gibbon views his own times. The outbreak of atavism in our last three decades and the awful destructiveness of two world wars make a passage such as the following, written in the last quarter of the eighteenth century, seem provincial and naïve: '[Man's] progress in the improvement and exercise of his mental and corporeal faculties has been irregular and various, infinitely slow in the beginning, and increasing by degrees with redoubled velocity; ages of laborious ascent have been followed by a moment of rapid downfall; and the several climates of the globe have felt the vicissitudes of light and darkness. Yet the experience of four thousand years should enlarge our hopes, and diminish our apprehensions; we cannot determine to what height the human species may aspire in their advances towards perfection; but it may safely be presumed that no people, unless the face of nature is changed, will relapse into their original barbarism.'[7] This passage was written at a time when the European calm may have seemed almost permanent. The last sentence implies a blindness on Gibbon's part to the possibility that civilization is merely a thin varnish which covers the barbarism in the heart of man.

[6] *The History of the Decline and Fall of the Roman Empire*, J. B. Bury, ed. (7 vols., London, 1896–1900), iv. 165.

[7] iv. 167–8.

Yet it is possible to acquit Gibbon for a good part of his optimism. Like Swift he thought of man as *rationis capax*, and he wrote the history of nations according to their use and abuse of reason. We are shocked in our day by genocide and by the incineration of modern warfare; but what are we to think of the Huns or of the Moguls as they appear in Gibbon's narrative? 'The destructive hostilities of Attila and the Huns have long since been elucidated by the example of Zingis and the Moguls; and in this more proper place I shall be content to observe that, from the Caspian to the Indus, they ruined a tract of many hundred miles, which was adorned with the habitations and labours of mankind, and that five centuries have not been sufficient to repair the ravages of four years.'[8] Gibbon's faith in the gradual progress of humanity towards perfection is at least not naïve; indeed, it rests on an extensive knowledge of the fierce passions of human nature, and on a keen awareness of how quickly civilized man becomes savage when he gives full reign to these passions.

We may apply to Gibbon, Taine's idea that the historian is a backward-looking prophet. It is not his predictive capacity that interests us, but rather his ability to discover through his study of the past significant understandings which may be applied to the present for a more meaningful interpretation of life. Although the questions Gibbon asks of the past are the questions of the Enlightenment, although the answers he discovers are those the Enlightenment expected, still within this context there is affirmed something of lasting value for mankind. Gibbon's *History of the Decline and Fall of the Roman Empire* is not only a document of major importance in the study of the mind of eighteenth-century Europe; the work is also a monument to the faith that man can, under conditions of freedom, and by the cultivation of his reason, civilize himself and his world.

[8] vii. 9.

INDEX

PRINTED IN GREAT BRITAIN
AT THE UNIVERSITY PRESS, OXFORD
BY VIVIAN RIDLER
PRINTER TO THE UNIVERSITY